Some OLD HOUSES in WESTBOROUGH MASSACHUSETTS and Their Occupants

WITH AN ACCOUNT OF THE
PARKMAN DIARIES

The Westborough Historical Society

HERITAGE BOOKS
2009

HERITAGE BOOKS
AN IMPRINT OF HERITAGE BOOKS, INC.

Books, CDs, and more—Worldwide

For our listing of thousands of titles see our website
at
www.HeritageBooks.com

A Facsimile Reprint
Published 2009 by
HERITAGE BOOKS, INC.
Publishing Division
100 Railroad Ave. #104
Westminster, Maryland 21157

Originally published 1906

— Publisher's Notice —
In reprints such as this, it is often not possible to remove blemishes from the original. We feel the contents of this book warrant its reissue despite these blemishes and hope you will agree and read it with pleasure.

International Standard Book Numbers
Paperbound: 978-0-7884-2129-7
Clothbound: 978-0-7884-8185-7

Contents.

Stephen Maynard and His House	3
The Simon Tainter House	12
The Samuel Forbush Tavern	15
The Parkman Parsonage	19
The Breck Parkman Shop	24
The Forbes Homestead	37
The Thomas Forbush House	43
The First Davis House	46
The Gershom Brigham House	48
The Haskell House	50
The Gale Tavern	54
The Thomas Whitney House	58
The Parkman Diaries	31
Additional Parkman Manuscripts	41

Stephen Maynard and His House.

Stephen Maynard was a man whose character was moulded by circumstances. He inherited without doubt from his Puritan ancestors his share of the New England conscience, but his life was so arranged that his conscience was left untrained. He had so many good traits and there was so little in his life to develop the bad that he had less need of a conscience, if you will pardon the expression, than a less prosperous, less kindly, less upright man would have had.

He had his full allotment of trouble before he had finished his life, but his boyhood was singularly happy. If nobility and breadth of character can be developed by broad expanses of green fields and blue skies, with forests of primeval trees and wooded hills and glimpses of river and lake, he had them all for daily seeing. There was nothing in the fair landscape spread on all sides around his father's home to suggest an unpleasant thought. This home, in itself unpretentious, was situated on the Lyman School Hill and the nearest buildings to it were the little church for which his father had given most of the land and the parsonage where Ebenezer Parkman, a rather young man, was bringing up in the best way his godly desire and conscience suggested, a large family of girls and boys.

Stephen's father and mother were among that class of people known as "the salt of the earth." Mr. Parkman, who surely must have known them as well as it is possible for one friend to know another, wrote a few words descriptive of each. The father he calls "a generous, bountiful friend" and speaks of his special kindness to the poor. Of Hepsibath, the mother, he writes:—"A woman of remarkable diligence and skill in family affairs and very compassionate and bountiful to the poor. A very serviceable person in our neighborhood and gave advice freely to all who sought to her." Perhaps no higher praise could have been written of a woman in the eighteenth century. We would expect that Stephen with the tendencies inherited from generations of godly forefathers would have developed just as he did and would have entirely deserved his father's written word—"my dutiful and well-beloved son Stephen."

Captain John Maynard, the father, was well-to-do; his lands of many acres he held in his right as proprietor of Marlborough, besides he had notes and bonds. Hepsibath Brigham, his wife, was a daughter of Samuel Brigham, the wealthy tanner of Marlborough, and she evidently brought to her husband lands which she had inherited from her father. Stephen was an only child as far as we know, certainly the only one who outlived his parents, and consequently the heir to their whole estate, a fact which in itself must have had a great influence on his character.

An only child is usually selfish, but if

Stephen Maynard was selfish, it was not after the manner of the weak who desire all good things for themselves, but after the manner of the strong, who grow masterful and carry their heads high with pride and take pleasure in bestowing of their abundance on others, not so much for the happiness they give as for what they receive in the consciousness of their high desert. His father was John Maynard Gentleman, he too was heir to that title, and it would not have been owing to any craven spirit on the part of his boy-mates or to any disagreeably proud way on his own part had he been acknowledged the leader in all the games and sports of the village. Perhaps it was only a development of this which made him, when still a young man, lieutenant in the King's army and later commander of all the troops in Westborough. Hence his later title of Captain.

His life can be divided into two distinct portions—the first comprising the years when he lived in the little one-story cottage still standing on Milk street, where it was moved many years ago; and the second after he built the mansion house by the Elsabeth river. We cannot draw the line by years between these two periods. In 1757 he was living in his father's house and there nine of his children were born, five of whom at least also died in this house as did also his wife, Thankful. At her death, in 1757, he was left with John, Antipas, Hepsibath probably, and Thankful, three days old. His wife Thankful was the daughter of Deacon Josiah Newton. It was a most suitable marriage. "She was a woman," writes Mr. Parkman, "who feared the Lord and had many excellent qualities." Recording her death Mr. Parkman notes in his diary that it was the seventh death in that house in 13 months. Stephen had lost his father, mother, wife and four of his children in that brief space of time, and the minister quotes, in view of these manifold afflictions a verse from one of the church hymns:—

> So teach us God! the uncertain sun
> Of our short day to mind,
> That to true wisdom all our hearts
> May ever be inclined.

Up to the dreadful summer of 1756 when death entered so many homes in Westborough and took away one after another of the children, Stephen Maynard's among them, his life must have been especially free from trouble. His father does not seem to have deeded any property to him or to have given up himself the care of his large farm as was the usual custom of that time. This may have been owing to the very active part that the son took in military affairs. We can picture him to ourselves with his scarlet coat with military trappings, the hat with gold lace and cord, the soldierly bearing and courteous manners, mingled sometimes with that decisiveness which made the minister feel that he was "too short" with him. The young men in Westborough eagerly responded to his many calls for troops. They felt proud to write, as did Constantine Hardy:—"I entered into His Majesty's service to serve my King and Country under Captain Stephen Maynard."

When the captain came home from the many trips to Crown Point and Ticonderoga and Canada which the long French and Indian wars necessitated, he was undoubtedly given a most flattering reception and made to feel that he was a great, if not the greatest man of the town.

At 37 he was probably at the height of his military prestige. Almost immediately after the many deaths in his family, there came the call of his country for his further service, and in less than three months he is getting a company together, with Thomas Parkman as drummer and Billy in the ranks—two of the minister's boys—to march against the enemy. He was gone most of the time for a year and apparently his first public appearance in Westborough after his return, was at the wedding of Miss Patty Death in November of 1758. This was on a Wednesday and the next Sunday Mr. Parkman noted that Captain Maynard and sundry others who have returned from the war were at meeting. We can almost see the flutter of the demure maidens, as they greeted the gallant captain on his return and the timid glances of admiration he inspired that November Sunday as he sat in his pew on the broad alley in the old arcade, handsome and confident and the envy perhaps of the younger but less attractive men.

He was quite in the habit of keeping his own counsel and he cared very little at the town's surprise when they heard published ten days later the marriage intentions of Captain Stephen Maynard and Mrs. Anna Brigham of Marlborough. They were married January 23, 1759, and drew their own lines as to who should be invited to the wedding, as we know from Mr. Parkman's entry for the next day. He writes;—"Mr. John Brigham of Sudbury (one-handed man) dind with me. Tells me Capt. Maynard and Mrs. Anne Brigham were married last night. Just before night I went over to Capt. Maynard's as he had desired, to meet him as bridegroom with his bride (his phrase was he then designed to bring home his wife). My wife did not incline to go, her child was very tendful and John was sick. *

* * It was also somewhat odd that our children were not invited to the welding (as neither were we ourselves) nor were any of them to this entertainment, though many others were not nearer related than they. But it is probable their thoughts were too much engaged to think much of this, so small affair. It was very cold, I walked there and returned o'foot. I left them at nine o'clock, omitting singing rather than run the venture of being too late." After all this self denial, however, he hears it reported a few days later on the street that he was there that night till one o'clock.

In six months Captain Maynard was in the army again and although he realized how very small was his father's little old house, as long as the war lasted, he could take little time to think of personal comfort, either for himself or for them. In 1763, peace was declared and with its declaration began the second period of Captain Maynard's life.

Between the time of his second marriage in January 1759 and the surrender of Canada to Great Britain February 10, 1763, which closed the French and Indian wars, probably several children had been born to them, although none are recorded in the Westborough Records, until 1768, when their daughter Elizabeth was born. His first boy, according to Mr. Parkman's diary, was born December 9, 1759. Benjamin Gott, Robert Breck, Stephen and Jeffrey Amherst, named for his old general, Lord Amherst, were without doubt his sons. Probably also Josiah. The records give no clue as to which was eldest. The marriages of three are recorded. Stephen was married first in 1783, when he would have been 24 had he been the first born, Benjamin Gott was married in 1787 and Jeffrey, under the curious name of Jepry Amhors in 1792. The only one whose death is mentioned is Stephen who died in 1806 but his age is not given.

Captain Maynard at the beginning of this second period in 1763 was 43 years old. Up to this time he had held no important positions in town affairs, his activity in the army had prevented this. He had however earned the honorable position which he now takes as counsellor and advisor. He was to serve the town as selectman and representative, to act on important committees and to be one of the trustees for the Indians. Having done all that he could to save the curse from falling upon his head which his Chaplain had graphically revealed to the army in his sermon from the text:—"Cursed be he that doeth the work of the Lord deceitfully and cursed be he that keepeth back his sword from blood," he was now enjoying his well-earned rest. It would seem as if for him the stress and tumult of life were over, and he could honestly say to his soul—"Take thine ease, eat, drink and be merry."

Here however we must pause a moment, to see if we can just what kind of a man the prosperous circumstances of his life had made of him. We cannot read many pages of Mr. Parkman's diary without concluding that he had inherited the gift of generosity which is mentioned as being a distinctive virtue of both his father and his mother. Presents of meat, cases of gin, etc., found their way to the parsonage with great frequency. At one time he undertook to straighten out one of the town roads at his own expense as Mr. Parkman records:—"Capt. Maynard solicits me about moving my walls on ye northwest and straightening the road from the meeting house to ye northward. He promises it shall not be to my damage. He will be at the charge and will measure the land that I may have equivalent."

He is ready also to do any small favors and we find him good-naturedly packing Billy Parkman's checked shirts in his valise when, in one of the campaigns, the troops have marched a few days before their captain.

His life seems to have engendered in him a desire to meet all expectations. He does not like to disappoint people either in a small way or a large way. In fact he liked to do a little more than was expected of him. When all his neighbors sent a load of wood to the parsonage, he would send three. As the richest man in Westborough, as his large estate made him, he had a certain ideal of living set before him by his townsmen which he wished to attain. He does not seem to have been a man who cared especially for his own comfort, but much for the good opinion of those around him.

He did not apparently take a very active part in the affairs of the church, although his wife Anna was a regular attendant.

It may be of interest to give an approximate idea of the property which he owned at the beginning of this second period of his life.

His father's original farm embraced the land on the Lyman School Hill to the Shrewsbury line. The northern bounds of this farm he extended in 1772 by purchase of the Tomlin farm just over the line in Northborough, better known as the Davis place. This farm added about 116 acres to the 400 in the homestead lot. In addition to this he owned 160 acres in Shrewsbury, also a farm near the meeting-house in Westborough which he probably inherited from his mother Hepsibath as it had formerly belonged to her father, Samuel Brigham This included a part of Memorial Cemetery, Mr. Parkman writes:— "March 29, 1759 N. B. A number of men at work in clearing some of Capt. Maynard's land and preparing it for the burying place. For ye fencing it some bring fencing stuff. Some are digging stones. I gave them a few Rodds of addition." This farm seems to have been northwest of Main street and extended from some point back of where the old Arcade stood, through the back line of Memorial cemetery. He also owned some lands in other towns.

Probably one of his first acts in this second period of his life was the beginning of the house on the Northborough road. He was entitled to the best house in town. He not only could afford it, but none other could grace it so well or make it mean so much to his fellow townsmen. We already know from Mr Parkman's remark about the seven deaths in the John Maynard house, that he was living with his father at the time of his wife's death, in 1758. We also know that very soon after this he was called to the war, that his second marriage took place in 1759, in one of his brief vacations at home and that a few months afterwards he was in the field again. Unfortunately, Mr. Parkman's most valuable Diary is lost for the years between 1761 and 1771. I think we may certainly say that the house was not built before 1761, for surely he would have mentioned it in the very full records he makes of matters much more trivial and which would probably have been of much less interest to him and his family.

The earliest allusion I have found to it in the Registry of Deeds at Worcester is in 1770. This paper is a mortgage for £400 of the certain messuage and tenement of housing where he then dwelt with houses and barns, to Joshua Loring. This mortgage was never discharged. It was perhaps given to defray part of the expense of building the house and was the first financial cloud which cast its shadow over his prosperity. He had previously mortgaged a part of the lot but not the part where the house stood.

According to the family tradition the house was seven years in building, which would be the exact number of years between the establishment of peace in 1763 and the placing of this mortgage when he was living in the house in 1770. The family tradition, which comes as do all the traditions in regard to the house from the descendants of Mrs. Maynard's daughter, Anna Brigham, claims that all the carved oak used in its construction was brought from England, and also that slaves built the stone wall running up the hill east of the house. Captain Maynard certainly owned three slaves at this time, a man with his wife and daughter, possibly others.

Most of you remember this house which stood until 1891, 14 years ago. To those who do not the picture in the possession of your society represents it accurately. The front door was on the northern side, leaving the eastern side, which was parallel with the Northborough road, for the living room. It may be of interest to many of you who perhaps never went into the house, and it may sometime be of value to the descendants of Stephen Maynard to have a few words of description of its interior. This I asked Mrs. Mabel G. Nourse, daughter of Mr. Bela J. Stone, who lived there during its last years, to write for me, and I will quote her exact words:

"As you opened the front door there were two rooms to the right and left, but no entry to speak of. The parlor was a large room with the large beam going across the ceiling, quite a fancy one. In fact the woodwork in that room was all fancy; in one corner was a very pretty open closet with shelves coming out in a round projection for bric-a-brac, etc., really a great ornament to the room. On the other side of the room were two closets, one quite small, the other larger, more of a clothes closet. The doors, as I remember, were large panels. Another large room used by us as a sitting room was directly back but had nothing remarkable about it aside from the large beam and wooden corners. Two doors led from this room into the dining-room, one through the back hall, the other by the little passage built into the chimney. By the way that chimney made itself very prominent in all the rooms. In the dining-room a large dish closet was built up against it. The rooms were low studded and all had the large beams. The house abounded in closets, in every conceivable place you would find one. The front stairway was paneled very nicely in banisters; at the head of them was a landing and a step each side to the rooms. The back stairs were directly opposite only very plain, closets and all. In the back room towards the street there were two little shelves set in the chimney and the largest of closets, inside of which was a small closet. There were four chambers right above the four lower rooms. Then in the attic were two rooms finished off and a large open space. The chimney looked as though at sometime there had been an open fireplace. I believe originally there had been a fence around the roof of the house."

Mrs. Nourse also adds that the hearth stone which used to be in the dining-room is now in front of the barn door. And there was in the kitchen a large square tank where the water ran constantly from a spring on the hill.

Captain Maynard never took the field again after the peace of 1763. He rendered most important services during the Revolution, but it was as counsellor not as soldier. Three of his sons served in the army: John, Stephen, Jr., and Benjamin Gott, John becoming a captain himself. Captain Maynard was at the breaking out of the war a man of 55. From 1768 through 1777 and again from 1785 through 1789 he represented the town in the legislature. He was a member in 1774 of the first and in 1775 of the second and third Provincial congresses. He served on Committees of Correspondence and in 1776 was appointed by special request from the Indians themselves one of the three trustees of the Hassanamisco Indians. Many of these Indians had probably served under him and they loved and trusted him.

Probably with so large a part of his life up to this time passed in camp and field, he had less knowledge of farming than most of his neighbors. Nearly all of them had received when attaining their majority some portion of their father's farms, and taken upon themselves thus early the responsibility of managing it. Stephen Maynard had received his land by inheritance when he was already a lieutenant in the King's army. Possibly farming did not suit his ideas of active life. We only know that he cast about in his mind for some other way of earning money than the farmer's way and decided to follow in the footsteps of his grandfather, Samuel Brigham, and become a tanner, or at least to make tanners of his sons.

In order to learn the art, he invited a young tanner from Rutland, Isaac Davis by name, to become a member of his family and impart his knowledge to them.

In 1772 Anna Brigham, the daughter of Mrs. Maynard, married Isaac Davis and they moved, according to family tradition, into the house which was lately owned by Hiram Broaders. Antipas, the captain's second son, a young man of 21, made his home with them.

John, the eldest son, was at this time married and living in Shrewsbury, leaving Antipas, the only remaining son of the captain's first marriage, to help him carry on this new business. Of his younger children, the eldest was now only a boy of 12, and undoubtedly the father was depending principally upon Antipas for developing and managing his share of the enterprise The records are silent as to the future of this son, but the family tradition again helps us out. According to it he left the Davis home one night, with his clothes tied in a hasty bundle, and for 12 years no word of him came back. Then there came a letter saying that his great desire to travel, for which he could not obtain his father's consent, had led him to leave. He had seen Spain and England and finally settled down to his trade of tanner in the Isle of Guernsey.

A few years ago papers were sent out by Clark University and other institutions of learning, with various questions to be answesed by those receiving them. They were sent in very large numbers to all classes of people and were on various subjects. Among others there was one on "Fear," and the question was asked, "What are you most afraid of?" When answered by women there was a variety in the replies. The men however gave almost all the same answer, that the fear which haunted them was the fear of being poor or of losing all they had and the power to get more.

This may have been—probably was—very far from Stephen Maynard's thoughts when he built his new home. It was built however, just at the beginning of one of the saddest financial conditions which has ever occurred in our country. To understand the calamity which overtook him in these last dozen years of his life it is necessary to look into the conditions then prevailing and the existing laws in regard to debt. During the Revolution, as you all know, the paper currency became greatly depreciated. The price paid for the necessaries and luxuries of life were abnormally high,—$50 for a handkerchief, $150 for a hat, etc. This was the greater burden to those who had to keep up appearances, who were accustomed to spend freely and who were called upon to help others and to finance to a greater or less degree all town and country enterprises. They were all looking for better times. In the meantime, in order to obtain the necessary ready money they contracted heavy debts. At the close of the war, the paper money had become utterly worthless. Prices were again low, lower than they had been for years. The debtors were the one class to suffer severely. The poor man who had spent but little found his small amount of money now went a long ways. But the debtor had no money, his lands were mortgaged, and the forced sales netted almost nothing. Like everything else they were almost valueless. After these sales had stripped a man whose property consisted almost entirely of land of them all and his debts were still unpaid, the sheriff had authority from the courts to seize his body and put it into jail where he was to be kept at the expense of the creditor until he was satisfied. Naturally under these circumstances, the debtor had but few comforts and no luxuries, unless provided by his family.

The records of the jail in Worcester are full of the names of Revolutionary soldiers, who, having served in the army with small pay and perhaps a large family at home to support, were unable to meet the demands of their creditors. Even Colonel Timothy Bigelow, who, throughout the whole war, was a colonel in active service, and who, like Captain Maynard, was a man of unusual wealth in 1775, was imprisoned in the Worcester jail for a rather small debt. from whence, as the quaint record says, he was "discharged by Deth."

There is a letter on file in the City Hall, in Worcester, which gives so pathetic a view of such a case, from one of these soldier's debtors, that I am sure you will pardon my quoting a few lines. This letter was addressed to the Selectmen of Worcester and was written by Nathan Johnson. He says:— "My disagreeable situation obliges me to take this method to acquaint you that in Consequence of my being taxed in this Town and not able to pay the same I am now confined in Goal where I have nothing to subsist upon only what I receive from my Charitable Friends," He then goes on to state that he is overtaxed and to describe how very fast his estate melted away by the fall of paper money and adds:—"This is therefore to Desire you Gentlemen to see that this Mistake is rectified and to Request your Interposition in Releasing me from my Confinement by setting me at liberty, giving me time to turn myself I will honestly pay every farthing that is due just as soon as I am able, but whilst I remain under Confinement I can pay nothing. I have no chance to turn myself."

This letter is dated April, 1784, and he wrote another similar to it in May. 1784.

It would seem that Nathan Johnson took a very common sense view of the situation, which might have appealed to many a creditor.

It was with this fate staring him in the face that Captain Maynard, hoping and praying for better times and a normal valuation of the financial medium then in use, saw his property gradually diminish in value until even his large estates were utterly insufficient to meet the debts which the exorbitant prices of the previous years had compelled him to contract.

At this time, only four days after Nathan Johnson was writing his second letter in the Worcester jail, Captain Maynard puts a second mortgage on his homestead, for £1283, Other property belonging to him was sold for debt.

This, however, was not all. He was holding, by special request, as we have seen, with two other trustees, the money which the Grafton Indians had received from the sale of their lands.

We find from the records of the Indian funds that this money he used as his own, expecting, without doubt, to be able to fully repay it. It amounted to over $1300, — "a desperate debt against Capt. Stephen Maynard," says the record, a debt which has never been paid and which the Indian Commissioner, in 1861, estimated would have been at that time $27,000.

Before judging Captain Maynard harshly for this course, I wish to call your attention once again to one of the laws in regard to debt.

According to the law of that day the spending of trust funds was not a felony any more than the failing to pay any other debt would have been. The laws usually represent pretty clearly the conscience of the time and, as we have seen, Stephen Maynard had had no experiences which would tend to develop his conscience to any higher plane than the common law

I do not think you would be especially interested in a list of the various mortgages and foreclosures, which seem so dry to us, and which were so vital to him.

He owed his misfortunes, I am sure you will all admit, to the unfortunate circumstances which prevailed. He had not made himself, as many a poor boy has had to do. He had been made by the fortunate circumstances of his birth. He was now overwhelmed by the unfortunate circumstances of the times.

Sometime in 1789 or 1790, he packed again for a journey, as he had done so many times in his soldier days. He said good-bye, as he had been wont to do, to his home and the dear town where he had always lived, feeling that it might be a last good-bye. He deeded his pews in the meeting-house, which were except from taxation, to his two sons.

It proved to be a last good-bye. As far as we know he never saw his beautiful home by the Elsabeth, nor the hills and meadows of his native town. We find him giving deeds of the little property in which he still had an interest, from a small town in Vermont, Barnard, in the County of Windsor.

His sons, Jeffrey, Amherst and Josiah, were with him, as we know from their being witnesses to papers which were made by him, as was also probably his wife and other members of his family.

I have not been able to learn when Captain Maynard died. His death is not recorded in Barnard. It is possible that he went with his old friend, Joseph Baker, who also left Westborough on account of his heavy debts, to Bakersfield, in Vermont. The town clerk of Barnard writes me that Maynard sold his property in Barnard in 1790, to a son-in-law of Joseph Baker's, an ancestor of his own. He remembers that his mother used to speak of Aunt Maynard who lived in Bakersfield.

He had died before 1796.

The house and homestead farm had been leased by the mortgagees to two men from Weston, Capt. Joseph and Lieut. Fortunatus Nichols before March, 1796 when it was sold to them by a Dr. James Lloyd of Boston. A month after this Anna, the widow of Capt. Stephen Maynard, releases for £100 all her right as "dower of widow's thirds" in the farm, and with this act the beautiful home passes entirely out of the hands of the Maynard family.

Nor did Anna herself long survive. She lived in Northborough after her husband's death, and died there July 6, 1799.

The inventory of her property shows pitifully how little she had bought since the beginning of the days of her adversity, how carefully she had mended and made over the old finery which had been the admiration of many of the young women of the town when she sat in her pew in the old church, just opposite Madame Parkman, or stepped into her coach at the church door and rolled down the Northborough road.

She had, according to this inventory, some notes, amounting to a few hundred pounds, three tables and 18 chairs, which were at Mrs. Parkman's, and her apparel.

The most expensive article in the list of apparel was a red quilt (petticoat) worth $1.50 Her bonnet of silk was worth 42 cents; her old velvet coat, 33 cents; her silk muff, 50 cents, and so on down a rather short list of things which once were choice and unusual, but now nearly valueless.

For nearly a hundred years after Captain Stephen Maynard stepped from his doorway for the last time, the house stood, an expression of his own character, as is every house which has been thought out carefully by him who is to live therein,—plain, substantial, hospitable, with kindly thought for other's comfort, a little larger, a little better, a little more beautiful than any other in town.

When its end came, it came suddenly. The house did not fall into decay, nor was it left uninhabited to suffer the inroads of old age in sight of every passer-by on the highway. Apparently it was just as solid, just as substantial, on the night of December 10, 1891, when it was entirely burned to the ground, as it had been in its early days.

HARRIETTE M. FORBES.
Worcester, January 16, 1906.

The Simon Tainter House.

The site of this house was in the grant to the heirs of Capt. Richard Beers in 1692. They sold to Samuel How and he, in 1698, to Thomas Rice, who, in 1725, deeded 60 acres of the "farm on Jack Straw's Hill at North part of same" to his son, Perez. Its north bound was "by Marlborough town line." In 1728, when a part of Sutton was set to Westborough, Perez Rice sold 80 acres including this site to Simon Tainter. He bought, in 1742, ten acres, "north of said Tainter's dwelling house," the south bound of which was "formerly Marlborough old line." In 1763, he deeded to his son Benjamin the farm of 111 acres, "together with the east and north parts of the dwelling house, the barn, mill house and all other buildings, except the west end of dwelling house from garret to cellar." This was evidently reserved for his own abode. In 1779, eighty-one acres with the buildings passed to Elisha Forbes.

He held it till 1807, when it was included in the 100 acres which he sold to John Wadsworth. After the latter's death in 1829, it was held by the widow Persis and the children until they sold their rights in 1855 to one of the sons, Cyrus, who in 1873 made over the farm to Cyrus Fay.

The owners since have been, Louis Pluff, Mrs. Cyrus Fay, J. F. Prescott, John and Anne Nestor, G. W. Nason, C E. S. McCorry, G. H. Burnham and W. A. Coburn, J. T. Costello and Alva W. York.

The house was built, we had thought, soon after the purchase of the land in 1728, but the Journal records April 1, 1726, "I rode as far as Mr. Tainter's to raising his barn. It was a somewhat pleasant time, but not altogether without Trouble and Toil" The date we have of its occupancy is 1737. Its style is familiar,—the two-storied front with long sloping roof in the rear, as in two other of the prints. The ell on the North side may have been a later addition. Over the front door was a tasteful gable with checkered moulding, as in the Breck Parkman house in the ell of the sleigh shop, Summer street.

This door opened into a small entry with its winding stairway. A large room was at either hand, low-studded, with corner posts and beams across the ceiling. Back of the north room was a bedroom and in its rear a large kitchen in the ell, reached by door and entry on the North side.

The south front room had peculiar cupboards, one above the other and between them a slide two feet deep. This was used for mixing the toddy and other liquors for the travellers that stopped on the way.

The chimney had its fireplaces with many cupboards built into the side spaces. It probably had its brick oven but this with set kettles was later in the ell. Just back of the front stairs and built into the chimney was a capacious dark closet with a narrow door. Its arched ceiling and walls were of brick. It was used by the elder Mrs Wadsworth for washing the dishes.

The south door opened into an entry with a woodshed at the left, through which one passed to the kitchen. On its inner side was a passage over a high platform to the other kitchen. Stairs from this led to the second story.

Up stairs were two large front rooms and one back of the north room. The south room was divided by a partition and in its rear was a store room. The attic was unfinished.

The floor boards were very wide and much more easily cared for than modern ones. The doors were made of like wide boards often without panels. A cellar was under house and ell with partitions.

We are indebted for the above details to Mrs. S. Maria Wadsworth, who lived here from 1867 to 1874.

The view from the front yard is of interest. Down the lane to the East was James Miller's house, used for storing hay when it was burned. Beyond Jack Straw Brook, on the hill south was the Daniel Forbes homestead with traces of cellar and well. The Barnabas Miller place was west of Ruggles street, marked by the old chimney. The house of M. Horatio Blake opposite Mt. Pleasant street has been moved toward the village. The blacksmith shop at the north corner of Eli Whitney street with the house of Mrs. Bayley back of it have passed away. Up that street just east of the Whitney house must have stood the Isaac Shattuck house of the early deeds,—its site now unknown.

The change that befell these neighboring dwellings came at last to the Tainter house and at midnight, May 23 1901, it was totally destroyed by fire. Happily a friendly hand secured in season a sketch of it and the picturesque appearance it presented with its dark weatherstained clapboarding with the light trimmings is finely preserved in the print before us.

The first occupant of the house was its builder, Simon Tainter. He was the grandson of Joseph Taynter, who in 1638, at the age of 25, came from England, in "Ye goode shipp ye Confidence of 200 tonnes." He made his home in Watertown. His youngest son Simon was "A man of means and was pious and charitable" filling many offices of trust. His eldest son was the Simon of our sketch. He was born in 1693. He married Rebecca Harrington in Watertown, where six of their children were born,—the other four in Westborough to which he came in 1726.

The esteem in which he was held is

13

seen in his election as moderator., assessor, purveyor of highways, and on various committees on school and other affairs. He was lieutenant in the militia.

Of his spiritual life, we get a glimpse in the record April 1, 1726 ' Simon Tainter (who had been with me some time ago) was with me in a very Heavenly and Devout Frame Conversing of his State and preparation for his admittance into the Communion." This occurred soon after.

He was deacon ten years, from 1757 to 1767. After his election Mr. Parkman wrote:—"I can't but look upon him as being all things considered, the suitablest person among us for said office, and hope God will graciously accept and reward him for his readiness to serve, he having in a distinguished manner a manifest Disposition and is very helpful to the poor and afflicted."

The Journal has scores of instances in which he assisted his pastor. Mrs. Forbes has so happily condensed many of these that we quote her words:—"inviting him and his wife to dinner when 'they had dressed a very large Pigg to entertain us' sending him fresh meat and wood, a bottle of Maderia, or a few oysters (in the shells) from Boston, selling divers sorts of edibles for Mrs. Parkman in the Boston markets, ploughing, sowing and reaping, and helping him in a thousand ways." With characteristic frankness, the minister had to confess, once:—"This important day for studying was greatly interrupted by both Mrs. Tainters who came to make cake and biskitt for my wife. Deacon Tainter and Daughter Warren here at Eveng. Their kindness and service verry acceptable had this been at another time." It was Mrs. Tainter who applied "a tobacco ointment" for the relief of her friend. In like spirit the deacon "takes his horse from his own ploughing and rides with me and goes to ploughing in my field."

He was the one to drive his minister to councils and had this record:—"I caut but take special notice of the Deacon's readiness to serve and waite upon me, in a very respectable manner and in the mean time is doing me the great kindness to subdue my new mare to drawing." He interested himself and his minister in the "sorrowful condition of the people at North Sutton." He had a mind of his own at times, for the minister records his "dispute with Deacon Tainter about the beginning of the Sabbath." His home was often the preaching place and at times was used for school teaching. In March 1767, the pastor's visits were daily to the sick one and on April 1, he "finds him very low." He died the next day aged 72 years.

In his will dated 1763, he left to his grandson Simon his silver cup and to the church some £6 and more, though the diary in 1780 refers to Deacon Tainter's legacy of £50 old tenor to this church.' His personal estate was inventoried at a little under £400.

Fortunate the man of whom it could be said:—"His duty was manifested by his high regard to the house of God, his constant attendance there, his esteem of the ordinance and ministers thereof. His deeds of charity were unstinted, his heart and hands being ever open to relieve and help, and to supply the necessitous, who now deplore the loss of such a friend and father."

It is well that we are to associate with this house one of such a character

The second occupant was his son Benjamin, to whom the father made over the farm four years before his own death.

At 21 years of age, the young man

was captured by the Indians at Adams, Mass. He was treated at first with great severity by his master whose brother he had shot. But later he was told that "for that cause he should claim him as an adopted brother."

When short of provisions on their hunting excursions, his master would go without saying as he drew his belt tight about him, "Indian can go without better than white man,"

Two years after captivity, he married Hannah Wood of Somers, Conn. He is often mentioned in the diary for his kindly services to the minister. He held the farm some 16 years, till nearly 60 years of age. One wrote of him:— "He owned a good farm but sold it for Continental money which proved of little value, migrated to Vermont, (June 20, 1780, with his sons and their wives and children) lived a short time at Newfane, Amherst, Mass., and Somers, Conn., returned to Vermont and lived with his sons Samuel and Ezekiel and Hannah Rice unto his death Aug. 1810, in his 86th year."

His grandson wrote:—"In appearance my grandfather was stern but was very pleasant and even in his ways and a devoted Christian."

The next owner was Elisha Forbes. He was the son of Daniel and grandson of the first Jonathan Forbes. He is often mentioned in the Diary and his relations with Mr. Parkman are akin to those of the Tainters, assisting in marketing the produce, caring for the troublesome sheep and "very generous with a number of presents." He married Hannah Flagg and had a family of eight children. He held the farm 28 years.

The fourth owner was John Wadsworth whose family owned the farm some 66 years so that it was often known as "The Wadsworth Place."

It would be of interest to trace as far as possible the families of the later owners. There is a work here that yet awaits to be done. It is enough if we have helped but a little to preserve, before it is too late, the remembrances of the older generations through the humble domicile in which they dwelt and toiled.

S. INGERSOLL BRIANT.
Westborough, Feb. 3, 1906.

The Samuel Forbush Tavern.

In 1671 the men of Marlborough began to wish for more extended dominion and sent a petition to the General Court asking for a grant of lands situated forty or fifty miles south west of Marlborough. The request was not granted so several of the young men took up farms in the western part of Marlborough, which was soon called Chauncy.

On Sunday the 26th of March, 1676, as the people were gathered in their meeting house, the Indians attacked the town of Marlborough. All the people but one, a Deacon Newton, reached the garrison house in safety, but when they came forth they found their meeting house and dwellings burned, their cattle killed and their farms ruined. Thus in a few short hours the result of their sixteen years of toil were wiped out. Disheartened and overcome by fear, the people left their lands and went to the older towns. But the death of King Philip, which occurred the next August, forever broke the power of the Indians in Massachusetts and two years later the town was again organized. The western part of the town grew quite rapidly and had a strong vote and inflence in town affairs. This growth was chiefly around Chauncy pond and the settlement came to be called Chauncy Village. When in 1688 Marlborough proposed to build a meeting house on the site of the one destroyed by the Indians, Chauncy people objected on the ground that it was too far away, and as this was now a strong community the town voted:—"That if the western part of the town shall see cause afterwards to build another meeting house, and find itself able to do so, and to maintain a minister. then the division to be made by a line at the cart-way at Stirrup Brook, where the Connecticut way now goeth. and to run a parallel line with the west line of the bounds of the town." This was practically the division later made.

For a quarter of a century the people toiled on, struggling with the problems incident to a new country, and now Chauncy begins to long for rights and privileges of its own. The natural conditions are favorable to growth, the only drawback being that the town is so far away. Accordingly, in the year 1702, a definite effort was made to found a new town. A petition was sent to the General Court based upon the vote of the town in 1688, already mentioned. This petition was not granted, and Chauncy remained for fifteen years longer a part of Marlboro. The subject of this sketch, Samuel Forbush, was one of the signers of this petition

Samuel Forbush, born in 1674, was the son of Daniel Forbush, who was born in Scotland in 1620. His wife was Abigail Rice. His brothers were Thomas Forbush and Jonathan Forbush, who was the first one of the family to write his name "Forbes." Samuel and Thomas and their descendants kept the name "Forbush."

Samuel Forbush was one of the original settlers of Westborough. He lived in the house now standing on the corner of Lyman and Oak streets. The house has been changed and enlarged since his day, but is probably the oldest in town.

There was a deed of $3\frac{1}{4}$ acres in Chauncy meadow given by Nathaniel Oak to Samuel Forbush in 1715.

In 1718, according to the town history, Samuel Forbush was appointed one of the committee "to wait upon the General Cort's Committee to Sett out the minister's Lot." Now, back in 1709 the Proprietors of Marlborough had set apart forty acres of upland and swamp west of Chauncy Pond and ten acres of meadow "at the west end of Great Middle Meadow," near Hobamoka pond as a "ministerial farm." The committee now appoined made an additional assignment of one hundred acres. This hundred acres was assigned to Mr. Daniel Elmer, who was the first minister of Westborough, though never settled. Upon leaving Westborough he sold the farm so Mr. Parkman had only the original fifty acres, together with such land as he bought for himself.

On the third of March of this year, 1718, was held the first of the "March meetings." At this meeting Samuel Forbush was chosen fence viewer.

In 1723 he served the town as one of the board of selectmen.

Early in the year 1729 Mr. Parkman was taken ill and was unable to attend to his pastoral duties for nearly a year and the town voted him £10 extra in spite of the "desents" of Samuel Fay and Samuel Forbush.

A deed given in 1732 names "Lieutenant" Samuel Forbush, and Parkman's diary in 1737 speaks of "Captain" Samuel Forbush.

He died in 1766, aged 92 years, and his will, presented for probate Dec. 15, 1767, deeds to Samuel Forbush, Jr., all real estate and buildings.

Samuel Forbush, Jr., seems not only to have inherited his father's name and estate, but also his public spirit. He served his town as a member of the board of selectmen for six years: 1773 and 4, 1787 and 8, 1791 and 2, and at the beginning of the Revolution War in 1776 he held the title of Captain.

In June, 1779, Mr. Parkman writes: "At eve, but before Sunsetting, I by Request of Mr. Samuel Forbush went to his House. He has been raising a new barn, and moving part of an Old One. I was at their Supper, after which we sang part of Psalm 112."

In December of 1779 the eighth entry in the "diary" says that Samuel Forbush came with his team and "brot Wood;" the tenth entry says he brought "old Wood, 2 Load;" the sixteenth entry says that he brought "more Wood." We get some idea of the value of wood in the early days from the remainder of the entry which reads: "Gave the former (Samuel Forbush) a Receipt for ten cord. He tells me ye Town voted to give 7£ per cord to Four of you 70£ apiece for 10 cord each." There seems to have been a lavish use of wood in the parsonage that winter, for in March Mr. Parkman says: "We are much reduced as to wood and the Weather is still too cold to be indifferent about it."

Deeds dated 1783 and 1790 mention land of Samuel Forbush.

In 1791 Samuel Forbush deeded to his son Isaac Forbush ¼ of 120 acres, of which twenty acres was the house lot. Its bounds were beginning at east corner by county road (now Oak street) near Cedar swamp, north and west by said swamp to Solomon Bathrick's, west by said Bathrick's to road, east by said road to beginning.

Isaac Forbush was born in 1758 in the old house and always resided there. For many years he conducted a general country store, and in 1803 was doing business under the firm name of Forbush & Warren, dealing in W. I. produce and the like. He was selectman in 1806.

The rest of the property of Samuel Forbush remained in his possession until his death in 1818. His will, filed Aug. 14, 1818, drawn up back in 1809, gives land ¼ to wife, ¼ to daughter, Lydia, ¼ to sons, Coolidge and Samuel—the latter two to receive all land at death of wife and daughter. It also gives to Zedida (late wife of my son Isaac) and grandson Lambert "that part of my land which now lyeth open to the road before my dores at the south and east end of my dwelling house, so long as she and he may keep a publick house of entertainment."

The "Forbush Tavern" now became the property of Lambert Forbush, born in 1789, the son of Isaac, the son of Samuel, the son of Samuel, the son of Samuel, the son of Daniel Forbush. In 1808 he married Rhoda Andrews, whose home was on the hill near where District No. 2 schoolhouse now stands.

Between 1806 and 1810 the Boston and Worcester turnpike was built.

This road between Roxbury and Worcester went, as all other turnpikes of that time, in a straight line. No hill was cut down or valley filled up. The coaches rushed up and down hill, some times crowded, a dozen people being inside and several on top. The fare from Worcester to Roxbury was two dollars.

When the coaches arrived, the hurry and excitement at the baiting places was great. They brought the outside world with all its news and budgets, past the little towns that had lived without it so long.

The Forbush Tavern was one of the "baiting places" at which stage drivers and teamsters stopped. Mr. Forbush was one of the best known landlords on the old stage route in Worcester County. He also had a very large farm and kept a large number of cows and sheep. The wearing apparel for the family was made from the wool which was spun and woven by the children. Flax was also raised on the farm, and the linen for the table cloths, sheets, etc., for the tavern, was made in the house. Twice a year, spring and fall, a shoemaker came to the inn to make shoes for the family.

In 1812 the soldiers enlisted for the war stayed for a while in Lambert Forbush's barn. When the roll was called one morning it was found that three men had managed to escape by digging out under the sills. They were captured and taken to Fort Warren, from which they again made their escape. One, Lovett Bixby, went to the Indians, where he married the chieftain's daughter. She was loaded down with rich ornaments which he soon succeeded in obtaining and then came back to his own kindred.

Lambert Forbush died in 1824.

In 1825 Lovett Peters, administrator of the estate, sold the property, 16 acres 125 rods including the dwelling house to Martin Bullard, the heirs with the widow, Rhoda (Andrews) Forbush assenting to the administrator's account. John Warren, Jr., was guardian of the heirs,

On the same day, Mar. 14, 1825, he deeds the above to Samuel Forbush, an uncle of Lambert. This Samuel Forbush was born in 1771. He conducted a large farm and also a market business, carrying beef, pork and other farm products to the Boston market. He held the office of selectman for the years 1816-19.

In 1823 there was a Restorationist Society in Shrewsbury, to which some Westborough people attached themselves, among them Samuel Forbush. He died in 1827.

On June 23, 1828, the heirs of Samuel Forbush, Orestes, Caleb, Lowell and Sally (wife of Edmund Harrington), deeded the whole estate to Elam Stearns for $3532 72.

For five years, beginning with 1820, the house was occupied as a tavern and post office by Captain Silas Wesson. At the end of that time he built a new tavern at Willow Park, now owned by the Lyman School. To this new building he removed his tavern business and post office.

Elam Stearns owned the place until early in the year 1832 when he committed suicide by hanging himself in the woods back of the house.

He left the place by his will, probated June 5, 1832, to Silas Howe, son of Luke Howe of Northboro.

In 1873 Silas Howe deeded it to N. Porter Brown and R. F. Bishop. In 1874 R. F. Bishop deeded his share to N. P. Brown, and in 1885 N. P. Brown deeded to Rev. Herman P. Fisher the house and land on the north side of the county road (Oak street) retaining for himself the barn and land on the south side.

The east side of the house is the old part. It contained originally, probably only six rooms. Later three rooms were added up-stairs. There was a large stone chimney in the middle of the house. On the front were probably nine windows, The door on the right side of the front hall led into the bar room, and the one on the left into the living room. Back of the living room was the dining room, and back of that the kitchen. One whole side of the kitchen was taken up by the large fire place, brick oven and set kettle.

The room over the bar was the dance hall and contained the only closet up stairs. It was a very large closet, extending the whole length of the stone chimney, and was probably used by the dancers for their wraps. The rooms over the living room and the three new rooms were sleeping rooms. The bar room contained the only closet down stairs. This was the toddy closet. This closet has been divided into three closets; one for books in the living room, one for dishes in the dining room and one for clothes in the old bar room.

In the corners of these rooms stand the square posts and across the middle of the ceilings run the wide beams. The walls are wainscoted. In one of the rooms the wainscot is a single board nearly three feet wide. The timbers of hewn oak are held together by oak pins. The nails used were made by hand. The old pounded latches are still on the doors. The west side of the house was built much later. The arrangement of the rooms is similar to that of the old part, but the marks of age, stone chimney, fire place, etc., are lacking.

The smaller barn back of the house was the private barn, only the family team being kept there, while the large barn across the road was the stage barn.

The place must have been well supplied with water as there are at least four wells around the house.

MATTIE L. FISHER.
Mar. 3, 1906.

The Parkman Parsonage.

Ebenezer Parkman was born in Boston, Sept. 5, 1703.

His father, William Parkman, was one of the original members and afterwards a ruling elder in the North Church in Boston, at the North End.

Ebenezer graduated at Harvard College, Cambridge, in 1721 and began to preach in 1723. We hear of him at Wrentham, Hopkinton and Worcester. On the 21st of Aug., 1724, he was waited upon in Boston, by a Mr. Shattuck, and invited to preach in Westborough. He accepted the invitation and came up a day or two later on horseback, leaving Watertown at 12.30 and reaching Westborough about dark. He preached the two following Sundays,—Aug. 25 and Sept. 1.

Journeys in those days were not only

tedious, but sometimes hazardous. The woods were stocked with something more fierce than the rabbits and partridges of these days. Nor were wild beasts the only inconvenience of the solitary traveller on horseback

Just at this time Indian hostilities were renewed, and the towns were full of nervous alarms. During his first visit Mr. Parkman walked to the meeting house from John Maynard's, Saturday afternoon, Aug. 31, with pistol in hand. At four o'clock an alarm was raised and the people rushed to arms, but happily no Indians appeared. On Tuesday, the first of Sept., 1724, a meeting was held of those who proposed to become members of the yet unorganized church and, on Friday following, they all called on Mr. Parkman, acquainting him with their proceedings and "their most happy union," and inquiring what he thought should be done farther. "They remained in conference" he said, "until sun down, and concluded with a prayer."

The young minister of those days had few advisers. His older brethren being in scattered parishes, and there being no means of easy assembly, he would be left to work out his problems alone.

But his mind was not wholly absorbed, even at this time, with the gravity of his position; there were sweets mingled with the sternness of his experience and while he consulted with the elders and read up on his duties, his heart was away at Cambridge, where a damsel of twenty-five summers, whom he knew, was busy with preparations for her wedding day.

Sunday over, and the consultations completed, he rode back to Boston, where a week later on Monday, Sept. 14, he was married to Mary, daughter of Samuel and Hannah Champney. With only a brief time for nuptial festivities, the young couple began preparations for their removal and settlement in Westborough and in less than a month were on the ground, and in their house.

On the 28th of Sept. a town meeting was held and it was voted to ordain Mr. Parkman as pastor of the church, and Wednesday, the 28th of Oct., was fixed as the time. The council met at Mr. Parkman's house, which stood near the rude meeting house in what was then known as Chauncy Village.

A covenant had already been prepared by Mr. Parkman. This had at a previous meeting been read, considered and signed by the candidates for church membership; twelve men, beside the pastor, who were to constitute the new church. There were no women in the church until the next July, when six were received; evidently the wives of some of the original members, including Mary, wife of Mr. Parkman.

In less than twenty years after the incorporation of the town of Westborough, the people began to bring forward the question of the division of the single town into two.

In Feb., 1744, Mr. Parkman recorded in his diary that he had received information that "a number of North side people met those of the South side, to gather subscriptions to a petition to the General Court that the town may be divided." This petition was presented to the General Court, and the result was that while no new town was then created, nor was to be for more than twenty years afterward, the North side was made a separate precinct, with power to elect its own officers, transact its local business and to constitute a separate parish, while the two precincts were to assemble for town meetings, to be held alternately in the meeting houses of each precinct. This was in 1744.

On the 22d of Jan., 1745, the people of the first precinct unanimously requested Mr. Parkman to remain their pastor.

In 1748 there was a proposal made to build a new meeting house and it was voted to build twenty-five or thirty rods easterly from the Burying Place. This was the old cemetery opposite the Town Hall.

Finally, the old meeting house was taken down, its materials were used in the structure of the new house, which in later years was familiarly known as the "Old Arcade."

Mr. Parkman still lived in the parsonage beside the site of the old meeting house, a little more than a mile away from the new one. On Sundays, he had not time to go home for his lunch between services, which was a great inconvenience, and as it was hardly consistent with the dignity that pertained to the office to carry it with him and eat it in the meeting house, and as no one offered to invite him in, he was obliged evidently to pay for his meal, for he petitioned the precinct to assume the expense of it, but at a meeting on the 28th of Nov. it refused the request.

This state of affairs necessitated the building of a new parsonage. "By deed of date, April 5, 1750," we quote from Mrs Forbes' notes in the Parkman Diary, "he had purchased the following described tract of land from Nathan Brigham of Southborough." "A certain tract of land measuring five acres and a hundred and twenty-six rods, situate on the Plain Northerly of the Burying Place in the first Parish in Westborough, Westerly of the road leading to Sutton and is bounded easterly and southerly by land left for a way & by Forty rods of land left for the Meeting House and four Rods for Stables, and likewise by the Burying Place. Westerly by the land of Capt. John Maynard, Northerly by sd Parkman's land & Northwesterly by Common land."

In Jan. the neighbors had met to break ground for the new house,—the spot occupied by the residence of the late Dr. William Curtis. The frame was not raised until the Sept. following and the building progressed very slowly. But the work was done thoroughly for the house is still standing just beyond the High Street School House; its oak timbers as sound as when first built.

"The house was well built and considered by some men extravagant, and Mr. Parkman himself records that he was criticized rather sharply by Dea. Tainter because his window frames were so large." "And although," writes Mr. Parkman, "I rebuked him for thus speaking, especially as there were many persons present, yet I was disturbed thereat; and the frames were larger than I intended, and I would rather they had been smaller."

The exterior of the house (aside from the "L" and the front entrance) the stairway and the two front rooms remained the same as when built until changed by the present owners.

The original house had on the ground floor, parlor, sitting-room, kitchen, summer breakfast-room, with fire places in each room. Above were five chambers, and two in the attic.

The "L" was built in 1800 and had a kitchen, a dresser on which shone Gen. Ward's pewter platters and bright copper tea kettles and skillets.

The original paneling remained in the front rooms, which were deemed "high finish" in those days.

When the house was moved to High street the "L" was sold to Michael Lane and moved to Willow street, and became his dwelling place.

"In the following August Mr. Parkman remarks in his Diary, he is obliged to move at once, although the house is unfit to be occupied,—the hearth is unlaid, the banks of gravel on each side of the door are unlevelled, and moreover there is no pasture for a cow, and no grass or hay for the horse. But move he must and the register, less reticent than he, tells us why. We find that he moved in on the 20th, and that on the 22d a child, Samuel, appeared upon the scene, keeping up the regular succession which for more than twenty years hardly failed to bring a new life into the parsonage once in two years." He had sixteen children in all, of whom only two died in infancy. For fifty-eight years, Mr. Parkman served as minister to the Westborough church.

For the town it covered the growth from the pioneer settlement, when Indians lurked in the woods and the roads were unbroken, to the day of schools and comfortable homes, and well tilled farms and strong civic life. When he came Chauncy Village had but just been included in the town of Westborough. It contained less than fifty families in an area nearly twice as large as it has at present. He had seen it grow to double its population and divide into two, and the southern town become as large as both had been at the time of division. He had ministered in the first meeting house during the whole of its existence and in the new one until it had become too small and had been enlarged and again overflowed.

In Sept., 1781, Mr. Parkman began to show signs of failing health. On the 16th of June, 1782, he wrote in his Diary, "It is fifty-eight years since I gave my answer to ye Town's call to ye ministry." "Few men," another has well said, "have ever been able to write such a sentence as that. . . . . For the man, it spanned all the years between the youth of twenty-one, fresh from his studies, preparing for his marriage and for the opening duties of his profession, to the old man of seventy-nine,—faculties failing, limbs growing weak and tottering; the whole of life behind him."

Rev. Elisha Rockwood says of him, "It is greatly to be regretted that no good portrait of him survives, to give us a clearer conception of the outward aspect of the man. His bearing was always in keeping with the honorable position he occupied. He magnified his calling, and was careful not to lower his dignity; but he was at the same time kindly and courteous. . . . He was, indeed, a bishop who believed that it was for the highest interest of his flock that they should be ruled, and he ruled them; but his sway was gentle and reasonable, and his assertion of his rights not so effectual as to prevent his suffering some inconvenience, and in his old age some actual want, through the neglect of those who were in duty bound to provide for his necessities. . . . The pages of his Diary are full of the lights and shadows of daily life, while pervaded by the sturdy and reverent faith of the men of his time. . . . His theology was such as the age produced. It could not be broad, for breadth of culture was an impossibility; but neither was it bigoted or unintelligent. . . . By his patient labors, in season and out of season, through times that tried men's souls, he and the men and women who toiled with him wrought out a noble beginning for those who came after him."

From a sermon preached on the 100th anniversary of the founding of the church we note the following item of interest:

"In the course of Mr. Parkman's long and useful ministry, 382 persons, including the first members, were received into his church; 1346 were baptized, and 260 couples were by him joined in marriage. By his records it appears that in the year 1740, a society of young men was formed for social prayer and religious improvement; and in the year following a society of young women consisting of thirty members, was formed to attend to religious exercises and catechetical instruction. And it is worthy of notice that this year, a greater number was added to the church, than in any other year except two, during Mr. Parkman's ministry.

Mr. Parkman died Dec. 9, 1782, and was buried in the present Memorial cemetery. A horizontal slab marks the grave and bears on it a noteworthy inscription.

After his decease the church was without a pastor for more than six years. Several candidates were heard and two of them, the Rev. Adoniram Judson, afterwards settled in Old Plymouth, and the Rev. Edward Mills of Sutton, were invited to settle; but want of unanimity in the choice, probably, induced them to decline.

But at length, in 1789, the Rev. John Robinson was consecrated to the pastoral office, which he held until 1807.

Feb. 28, 1789, the heirs of Mr. Parkman deeded their rights in his estate to Elijah Brigham, who had married in 1780, Anna Sophia, the daughter of the minister, and had lived in the parsonage. He continued to live there so that it has generally been known as the "Judge Brigham" house.

He served Westborough for many years as representative, senator and councillor. For sixteen years he was judge of the Court of Common Pleas for Worcester County. He was elected to congress in 1810 and was a member of that body until his death in 1818.

His third wife was daughter of the famous patriot, Gen. Artemas Ward of Shrewsbury.

On Dec. 30, 1839, the heirs of Judge Brigham deeded the estate to Orlando Leland, — "the principal part of what was set to the widow as her dower." 61 acres 25 rods

Sept. 24, 1851, Orlando Leland sold the same to Reuben G. Holmes whose death occurred last January.

On July 24, 1858, William Dickinson, the assignee of Mr. Holmes, deeded it to Edwin H. Lovell. Mr. Lovell, Oct. 22, 1862, deeded the same to Jonas and Lewis Rice.

The Messrs. Rice, Jan. 17, 1867, sold it to Dr. William Curtis, who moved the house to its present location, in order to make room for his new mansion.

On April 14, 1887, the executors of Dr. Curtis sold the house and land to Joseph Smith, who on Sept. 23, 1903, deeded it to Mrs. E. T. Pierce and Miss Cora Taft, the present owners.

     LOUISE S. KELLEY.
April 9, 1906.

The Breck Parkman Shop.

It is only just to those who have gathered so much valuable material from the scattered journals of the Rev. Ebenezer Parkman, to say publicly, that these from which I shall quote tonight have not been purposely withheld. They descended to my mother from her uncle, Robert Breck Parkman, grandson of the Rev. Ebenezer.

Realizing their value to her, and fearing that at my death they might fall into strange hands and be critcized through ignorance, I carefully wrapped and hid them, some years since, with written request that they be "burned without opening."

When this paper was suggested I bethought myself of this hidden treasure. Turning to it I found a mine of valuable information, before unknown, just a little of which it is my privilege to bring to you.

The Rev. Ebenezer Parkman was the grandson of Thomas Parkman of Sydmouth, old England, and son of William Parkman of Devonshire. He was born in Boston, Sept. 5, 1703. In 1724 he married Mary Champney of Cambridge. To them were born five children, Mary, Ebenezer, Thomas, Lydia and Lucy. Mrs. Parkman died after an illness of about a week, Jan. 29, 1736.

In Sept. 1737, he married Hannah Breck, of Marlboro. To them were born 11 children. Elizabeth, William, Sarah, Susannah, Alexander, Breck, Samuel, John, Anna Sophia, Hannah and Elias.

(Of Mr. Parkman's lineal descendants there are are now living six great grandchildren and 14 great-great-grandchildren.)

Madam Parkman (Hannah Breck) was one of my intimate acquaintances in my girlhood days, notwithstanding she died in 1801 and I was born many years later.

Her portrait stood in our attic for many years, for age debarred it from the better rooms of the home. It was in a black frame and was itself a black and white painting, without light or shade, representing a very masculine woman. Her hair was well covered with a ruffled cap, extending under her chin Her sleeves finished at the elbows, with ruffles. Her cheeks were hollow, her mouth large, set in expression and speaking reproof and displeasure. Whichever way I turned and in all my most innocent play, her look of cold disapproval followed me. rousing my dislike to such a degree that I spent many hours in looking her out of countenance and making faces at her, which I am glad to say my mother never knew. Her portrait, with that of her son Breck and his wife, was given to my uncle, Dr. John E. Tyler, for many years superintendent of the McLean asylum, and is still in the possession of Miss Denny of Boston.

Breck Parkman, her sixth child, was born in the parsonage at Wessonville, Thursday morning, Jan. 27, 1749. He bore the family name of his mother.

His youth was spent in farming and learning the carpenters' trade. We find him in Dec. 1771, at work for himself in the shop. In March 1772, he finished his school and returned home. In April, he plans to set up a store, for he is in some perplexity about Mr. David Hills coming to set up trading in the neighborhood. He also hears of one Mr Gillam Bass of Boston hiring a part of Deacon Wood's house and designing to open a shop of goods there, and tries to dissuade him. April 25, he is preparing the shop, putting up shelves to receive goods. He goes to Boston for goods and settles his shop, marking his goods, etc. May 5 he has customers flocking to him. There is an interesting account of the rivalry between the traders. The parson's indignation and reconciliation to Mr. Bass and family, are of interest.

On Aug. 28, 1772, is a record of the building of the shop, which is the subject of this sketch. Having secured the consent of the proprietors of the adjoining stables, "a number of hands (to 40) came together and moved the stables aforesaid—and the shop—and raised a store 35 feet long but 8 feet post. No disaster. D. G." Sept. 7, workmen are closing, digging, stoning, etc.

From the journal of June 1773 to July 1775, we find him interested in the purchase of goods and in this modest store which stood on the land purchased by his father in 1750 from Nathan Brigham of Southborough.

On June 24, Mr. Parkman makes mention of the shop when he writes: "Reckoned with Breck and paid him his Book Debt." Breck was at this time 24 years old. "My son John at work for Breck making a house for him. Mr. Spring works on the little house to the value of 7 shillings, 6 pence, old tenor.

Mr. Fisher here to make the bench of the little house but not the partition from the rest of the house."

In August, mention is made of Miss Susie Brigham, whom Breck afterwards marries, as at work for Mrs. Kelley, also makes a gown for Mrs. Baldwin. She undertakes to make a DuCape for Mrs. Parkman. Later she made sundry gowns, stayed after meeting, lodged. worked for Sophy and Hannah in making new crape gowns.

In Sept. Sophy is at Breck's shop Breck returns from Mendon with the Vendue of the Wilder goods. In Oct. Breck has hired Mr. Jacob Snow to work for him in building a pew in the meeting house; with him Joshua Chamberlain and they diet here. Breck in the afternoon sets out for Boston. Returned at evening Says he saw a poor criminal hanged. The crime was Burglary. His name was Levi Ames. O! that the others might take warning, hear and fear, and do no more so wickedly.

Elias goes to Mr. Whipple's mill with a team loaded with salt to be ground, 25 bushels, for his brother, Breck.

Breck and a number met at Lieut. Baker's in order to unite in a society to collect a library of useful books.

January 1774, Breck and John ride on the sleigh to Shrewsbury and return. An exceedingly cold season. My son John at the Ministerial Lot cutting wood and sledding from thence.

The snow very deep. Mr. Hancock sledding for Breck. Extremely cold: too cold for John to sled wood, having already his heels froze, and Ben Clark two fingers. Extremely cold. Susie Brigham lodged here last night, Breck, John and Hannah ride in a sleigh to Boston. Breck hires Mr. Joseph Bond to go to the Ministerial Lot, breaking the way to Mr. Beeton's for a Load.

At evening John Fay here and lodged in Breck's Store. My lane back of the Meeting House so full of snow banked up and blown compact and hard, that there is no passing but upon it.

At evening Breck and John returned from Boston.

March. Both Breck and Susie ill last night and droop today.

Breck goes to Wrentham—returns, and acquaints me with having hired a man to work for me for six months.

April. Miss Susie Brigham here from Day to Day, assisting Sophy in her work.

Breck assists in filling, loading, and emptying Goods. Breck nigh evening goes home with Susie Brigham. Breck went for Mr. Morse to Northborough and Shrewsbury for Gloves, etc. in preparation for the funeral of Mrs. Morse.

Mr. Fisher came again to his work, had also Mr. Moses Sever to work at the wall on which the new fence is erected,

Breck returns from Boston. He tells me he went to see my Brother, who is more and more infirm. An awful Superannuation.

O! that I might be useful while I live, and ready and willing when God shall call me.

July. Breck goes to Military meeting at Lieut. Baker's who I hear chose one of the Captains to settle their affairs. Breck has a large company who stop at his store. Breck paints the sign of the Blue Anchor for Dea Wood.

August. The Town met again on the affair of subscribing the agreement. I am informed that my son Breck found it necessary to subscribe.

My son Breck has caused Joseph Cullock to come to my work of laying the wall leading Northerly from the Store.

Breck goes to Lancaster for Trees, returns and relates what John met with from a Thief. who lodged in the same chamber. at Mr. Lock's Tavern in Lancaster. Picked his pocket, and carried away two Pocket Books.—but he recovered them, and the Thief was put in Worcester Jail.

Sept. My son Breck with provisions, Bread, Meat, etc., Coats, Blankets, etc., for it was rainy,—rides down toward Cambridge to relieve Asa Ware. Mr. Spring and others who were unprovided.

Dec. Miss Susie Brigham here still. Miss Abigail Woods works for Breck making clothes for him—but diets and lodges here. Breck goes to Lancaster. Am concerned about Breck, who does not come home till late. Difficult weather, and night dark, till at length he came, with his Mare in hand, strangely and suddenly distempered. Mr. Benjamin Willard, Clock Maker, dined here.

January, 1775. We had uncommon trouble today in breaking a way to the Ministerial Lot—Breck very much fatigued.

Susie Brigham here—(a month later) here with Miss Abbie White stayed over night—(a month later) continues here making stays.

Mr. Saml Fay very much disturbed with me that I don't make my son Breck pay him for his dead Mare, or turn him out of doors if he will not. Such was the unreasonableness of his conversation with me, and that he would not come to Meeting until he had satisfaction.

At an adjourned church Meeting the Committee from Mr. Fay reported that he was greatly offended with me because I kept my son Breck. I made a short speech. It was put to vote but no stand up. Nothing was done. Adjourned for two weeks.

Breck went to Mr. Samuel Fay's and tried to make up with him. Had Dea.

Wood to assist him in it, but in vain.

April. Sophy keeps Breck's shop herself, neither did anybody lodge in the store last night.

Agreed with Aaron Warrin to live with me and do my work, for six months, for £75, old tenor, and I am to let him have a few things out of my son's shop pretty soon, also, some money if he shall need it, when he has earned it.

Sophy had a letter from Breck that he inclines to list but has not. He thinks to return home.

Susie Brigham came last night which made the ninth person beside my own family. So today we are 13.

Much that the missing pages contain would greatly enhance our story, but there is much which we may conjecture; for during those 21 months the store, which had been enlarged from time to time, had come to be known far and near as "Breck Parkman's Shop." Its proprietor was now 28 years old, and was not only striving to enlarge his business, but was dreaming of a young girl in Northborough, whose charms had so engrossed his thought, and his heart, that the serious question of marriage was mingled with all his daily toil.

His hopes were not without foundation for Miss Susie Brigham already loved Breck and was ready to enter life's path with him. They were married by the Rev. Peter Whitney of Northborough, Jan. 9th, 1777. The bride was 23 years old.

At the beginning of the remaining journal, Sept. 3, 1777 to Oct. 31, 1780, we find Breck setting up his clock bought at Vendue at Boston.

This clock dates back to the year, 1768, or thereabouts, and was made by Edward Clarke of No. 9, Holburn, England.

How much of history its hands recorded as it measured the weeks and days of 48 years in the "best room" of the happy young couple, we may never read. In its quiet faithfulness it welcomed and watched over the seven children whom God sent to gladden their home,—all of whom followed in the footsteps of their honored parents and grandparents.

It was the property of Breck Parkman until his death in 1825. It then went to his son, Robert Breck; at his death, in 1855, to his sister, Charlotte Sophia Parkman, wife of Hon. George Denny of Boston; at her death to Augusta Maria Denny and her husband, Dr. John Eugene Tyler, Jr., both grandchildren of Breck Parkman, and in 1900 descended to Robert Breck Denny of Boston.

The present owner sets priceless value on this heir-loom, and for his own pastime wrote the following verses, which are pasted on the inside of the long door:

TO THE OLD PARKMAN CLOCK
Faithfully for one hundred years
You've pealed the hours away
Unmindful of the joys or tears
Allotted to each day.

Three generations' story told!
Now steady as of yore
You tick the seconds clear and bold
The same as heretofore.

How little did your maker dream
Your works would run so well,
Or ship could sail on seas serene,
Without a storm or swell.

Much less he thought of future praise,
As skillfully he formed
Those patient wheels in by-gone days,
That have this race performed.

Unnumbered months will fly apace,
Still with a measured beat,
Time's record on your placid face,
With watchful care you'll keep.
R. B. D.

I would say that these lines were written by Mr. Denny without thought that they would be given to the public, but the veneration they express, not only for the old clock, but for our ancestors is worthy of Record.

Returning to our journal of Sept., 1777, we read: Breck obliged to ride at evening to Major Champney's, at Southborough, on account of commissions to be brought to this Town. Breck returns from the Army in the West and has endured his excursion considerably well. Thanks to God for His favor. Many people going over the Post Road to see the Regulars in their moving toward Boston. Breck, Susie, Elias and Sophie ride there. Gov. Burgoyne's Army are expected to be on their road to Boston. We are disappointed in the Worcester Spy; nobody goes for it. Mr. Howe dines here, being at work for Breck. Breck papers his lesser room and Elias helps him in the p. m. and evening. Breck sets out for Hartford on public Business. Susie having a Horse from her Father, and Sophie with Breck's mare, rode away (tho' a cold season) to Leicester, designing to visit farther. Breck returns from Lebanon.

March, 1778: Breck makes a business of Book Binding, especially Singing Books.

April: I went to the ministerial lot, for Breck is getting timber there for a back room to his store. Breck has raised a leanto additional to his store, dimensions 27 by 12 ft.

May: Mr. Lamson at work for Breck on his additional building. Breck with Mr. Lamson shingles the roof of his new Store. Mr. Lamson & Mr. Jonathan Batherick at work with Breck in boarding the sides of his additional building.

June: Mr. Moses Nurse having brought a load of Earthen Ware from Danvers to Breck's store, I took the opportunity to give him solemn admonition and charge concerning his absence from the House of God. Breck met with disaster by his stairs into the upper story being shocked, the supporting timbers being thrown down. Breck informed me that Mr. David Stowe's son was at the shop.

Oct. 22, 1778: About three in the morning we were alarmed by Breck, Susie being in travel. Near Sunrise a little daughter was born. Both mother and child in a hopeful state. All glory to God the Deliverer—and may his glory be perfected.

Sunday afternoon in consideration of the baptism of Breck's child, I preached on Gal. 3:14: "That the blessing of Abraham might come on the Gentiles through Jesus Christ:—that we might receive the promise of the Spirit through faith."

The child was called Hannah Breck. At eve went down to Breck's and had our evening exercise there. May God graciously accept us in these various solemnities, and may the blessing of Abraham descend on us through Christ.

This child was my grandmother.

She married Dr. John Eugene Tyler of Mendon and Boston, who was one of the original organizers and first deacons of Park St. church. At his death she moved to Westborough with her five children and lived in the home of her father, Breck Parkman, until her death in 1834.

In 1781, Susannah, the second child of Breck and Hannah Parkman was born and in 1809 she married the Rev. Elisha Rockwood, who was pastor of the Congregational church in Westborough for 27 years.

Up to this time the "old shop," with all the additions and alterations we have noted, was rapidly growing too small for increasing business.

This, with the advent of two daughters into the house, made the question of larger accommodations a stern necessity. What should be done was the burden of their thought and prayer, for to build with their limited means meant greater sacrifice than they had yet known. But they were young and strong, and bound together by a love which could overcome all obstacles and through which, with God's help and leading, (for He was a partner in all their interests) the decision to build was fast culminating.

Doubtless the good father appreciated their increasing need, for we find that in Nov 4, 1782, he deeded the lot (209 square rods) and the store to his son Breck. This lot lay east from the meeting house, 45 feet distant, while the store corner was 10 feet farther east on the front of the lot.

Already, as early as May 29, the record reads, "Breck is moving the stables, granery and necessary office that he may prepare the ground for his building an house." This was raised July 10, and stood between the shop and the parsonage. It was 28 feet front and 30 feet back. "Through the goodness of God there was no evil occurrent. One hundred and 15 persons were entertained." Aug. 6, workmen are daily boarding and closing. Oct. 8, Breck's mason lays the foundation of his chimneys.

This house was later moved and became the ell of the sleigh shop on Summer street. I imagine it was a very plain structure without any of the conveniences which we of today demand as necessities. But the peace of true love, with the greater peace of God, "which passeth all understanding," dwelt there, all of which made life look very bright to them.

Into this home were born five children, Charles, Robert Breck, of whom I may speak later, Anna called Nancy, Mary Augusta, and Charlotte Sophia, born in 1800—she being the youngest—while my grandmother, Hannah Breck, was the eldest of the children.

Business still continued in the old store, which we have seen enlarged by the addition of rooms heretofore occupied by the family. Subsequently a partnership was formed with Judge Brigham, a brother-in-law of Breck's. We have a day book, dating from Mar. 3, 1792, to April, 1794, with account of sales,—the initials P. & B. (Parkman & Brigham) gracing the first page.

The first charge was to Jeduthun Fay for "Sugar, Rum, tow cloth and molasses." There were also charges for "Rice, Biscuit, Tea, Powder, Shott, chalk, iron, handkerchiefs, Buttons, Shawls, Lawn, Wine, Glass, stockings, West India Rum, Brandy, Eggs, Redwood. Files, Twist," etc., etc. The variety of articles kept for sale was greater than that of the present department stores, as we shall see. Nails were also sold by the hundred; one charge a hundred for 10 pence. Could this be the origin of the name given to a certain size nail called "ten penny nail?"

Following the list of articles kept, we find "Shoes, Hats, Bottles, crockery, Bibles, Spelling Books, Writing Paper, Blank Books, Sole Leather, Boards, Shingles, Harnesses, Veal, Pork, Butter, cheese, N. E. Rum, Buckles, Shalloon, Buckram, Fustian, teapots, candlesticks, Flour."

Somewhere between the years of 1794 and 1798, Parkman & Brigham built a store on the south side of Main street, which at the writing of the History of Westborough stood in the rear of Central block, where they attended to business for a time. Later the partnership was dissolved, when Elijah Brigham became a member of congress. He died in Washington Dec. 22, 1818. Our journal says he was greatly lamented, "highly respected in his death, and honored at his funeral." A monument was erected to his memory in Washington.

Breck Parkman continued business in the store already noted on the south side of Main street until 1798—when he erected a long, low, two-story building on the west side of Main street, where the present Postoffice block now stands.

At this time his two sons, Charles and Robert Breck, aged 13 and 11 years, were, doubtless, showing boyish interest in the store, and gave promise to the fond father that some day they would take his place. With this in mind he watched their growth to maturity and to the consummation of his anticipations.

He died in 1825, at the age of 76 years. He gave directions about his funeral, told where to obtain boards for his coffin, etc. He died perfectly resigned with strong faith in Christ.

At his death the management of the business fell to his oldest son, Charles, who later owned and lived in the house which stood on the present site of the Whitney House. He had eight children, one of whom, Mrs. Maria Denny Parkman Leach, survives him.

By the father's will, allowed in 1825, the dwelling house, the Nourse place and all lands between, were left to his son, Robert Breck. He was a bachelor, of singularly nervous temperament. Notwithstanding his peculiarities he was a godly man of much faith and prayer. He died in Hartford, Conn., in 1855.

At the death of Charles, in 1834, his son, Charles Breck Parkman, succeeded him in the business. After superintending it for a few years, his interest turned toward the west and he later located in Indianapolis, where he died in 1885.

Many were the proprietors of the old Parkman store during the next 35 years, men of sterling principles and marked business ability, of whom much might justly be written.

On the night of March 20, 1868, this ancient landmark was totally destroyed by fire. The next year the present Postoffice block was erected on its site.

In 1835, "Breck" (as he was called) had deeded to his nephew, Charles Breck Parkman, "all right to the real estate devised to me by my father, Breck Parkman, of any description."

On a map of 1837, the shop stands in the name of C. B. Parkman. In 1842, it passed to Rufus Harris, 1¼ acres. In 1853, R. Harris sold the shop and lot west of it to A. Davenport, A. J. Burnap and A. M. Howe.

Could we open the pages of history which time has written, our story would read like a tale of fiction. But they are sealed. The withering grasp of age had so defaced our once honored shop that it could no longer grace the Beacon street of Westborough. Hence, it was removed about 1855 to the south side of Summer street, to the site now occupied by the Nourse trellis factory. It there served as a dwelling house for George L. Bannister and Mrs. Annette Bullard (now Dudley).

In 1863, it was put on wheels and carried to Milk street, near site of the Gould & Walker factory, but before it was unloaded it was bought by Patrick Cronican and on May 5, 1863, was moved to its present site at corner of South and Cedar streets.

Through the kindness of its present owner, Mrs. Bridget T. Cronican, I was permitted, a few days since, to examine the old house, with the hope that some initials or figures cut into the wood might be found which would give a word from out of the long ago,—but the accumulations of years had obliterated every vestige, only the old stairs and main beams proved its advanced age.

The old part of the house consists of three rooms and a small front hall. Through the courtesy of Mr. Cronican, I have a plan of it, which anyone interested can examine, and which as a society we should hold amongst our valued papers.

The Parkman Diaries.

From the journals referred to in the foregoing article, I want to give you Mr. Parkman's account of a journey on horseback to New Haven, Conn., and return, with his bride Hannah Breck, in Sept. 1738, the year following their marriage.

The previous June of the same year he writes: My honored and aged Mother undertakes a journey to Westboro with me. My wife riding single, and my Mother behind me. We changed horses, and by that means my Mother had a very comfortable journey, and we got up in good season, through the great goodness of God. Later, he adds, my Mother in great comfort returned home. When she took her leave of my family, and blessed them, among other of her expressions, this was remarkable: She kissed my two Sons, saying, "God Almighty bless the Lady, and make them a Blessing."

Sept. 6th. About nine this morning my wife and I sat out upon our Journey to Springfield and New Haven, on my own, and cousin Winchester's horses. Mr. Tainter bore me company to Mr. Cushing's. Dined seasonably and comfortably at Col. Chandler's at Worcester.

P. M. rode to Richardson's at Brookfield by about quarter after five. The Richardsons were heretofore Malden Milk-folks to our family at Boston. They were very obliging, and would receive no pay for our Oats. We got to Mr. Cheney's a little before candle light, but were so unhappy as to find neither Mr. Cheney nor Madam at home. Mr. Cheney was gone to wait upon a number of Gentlemen who were upon the Road. We tarried with Mrs. Dolly Hawley. Dr. Pynchon of Springfield came in and tarried over night likewise.

In the morning about three quarters after eight, we sat out with Dr. Pynchon's company. At half after one arrived, weary and tired, at Scott's, in Kingston. Dined there. Left Scott's at half past two. One Mr. Ball of Springfield, an Irishman, bound to Glascow, added to the company. At Lamb's in Springfield at half after three. Norwich Indians there. Left at twenty minutes after four. Mr. Breck met us a little before we got to Town. Arrived by day-light, and not as tired as last night.

8th. Rainy Day. The heavy showers were a great Blessing, it having been at a Time when there had been an unusual Drought.

9th. Fair, bright day. I waited upon Col. Wm. Pynchon after I had viewed the River, and the Burying Place. Some remarkable inscriptions. Whilst we were at Col. Pynchon's with President Holyoke, Mr. Williams of Longmeadow came and after him Mr. Hopkins of the other Parish. They shaped a scheme for my preaching at the West side, which I consented to.

10th. Sunday. In the morning I crossed the River, and went up to Mr. Hopkin's. The first and second Drum beating to give notice to the People.

Preached on Luke 16:23. The women all sat on the wrong side of the Meeting House. Deacon Parsons very courteous to me, and walked with me to the ferry at evening. Cold night.

Mr. Holyoke and some number besides, were going up to Mt. Tom (called so, as tradition has it, from one Rowland Thomas) and to Mt. Holyoke (called so from one of the President't ancestors). But we rode to Longmeadow when the Frost of this morning which was very great was in a great degree gone.

Mr. Williams, our Guide to the Suffield Ferry. We crossed the Ferry and rode to Mr. Devotions at Suffield. A fine prospect on the North of Suffield meeting house. After kind entertainment, dining, etc., set out in the middle of the afternoon, rode to Windsor and Hartford, and were kindly entertained at Mr. Austin's.

500 Hogsheads of Tobacco shipped off last year from the Connecticut River, to the West Indies, and chiefly from Windsor.

In Wallingford, or North Haven, a Vessel building some miles from the Water. Cornfield five miles long.

A late sorrowful occurrence by thunder:—the Steeple shivered, a man thrown down from it and killed. Four persons buried in the Highway for Suicide.

Pleasant fields on the North East side of the Mountain. Stopped in North Haven. Called first at old Minister Pierpont's. College illuminated, seen two miles off. Mr. Edwards of North Hampton came to see me and walked with me to College. Several friends came in to see us at going off. Mr. and Mrs. Pierpont went some miles with us, Mr. Daniel Edwards and Mr. Belden of Norwalk were our company. Sorrowful leave taking of our friends.

Dined at Hall's in Merryden, a corner of Farmington (as I remember), at three quarters after one. Set out again just an hour after. Halted at Wethersfield in the evening, and then though wearied and tired, we stood it out to Mr. Sec. Wyllis's in Hartford.

In the morning proceeded on our journey. One of our Horses blundered overboard of the Ferry Boat, wet the side saddle, etc., but we received not much more Damage than the hinderance thereby. Our great suspense whether we should ride to Springfield, to which place we decided to go. Mr. Wyllis and Mr. Ellery accompanyed us as far as Grant's Tavern, where we dined, oated, etc., and all at their expense. Arrived at Mr. Brock's a little before day light down; nor were we so tired as at some other times. Mr. Brock rode with us two or three miles. Dined at Scott's.

Lost our way and wandered some time, but found our road so seasonably as to get to Mr. Cheney's in the first of the evening. Were cheerfully received and handsomely lodged.

Sat out the next morning from Brookfield. Dined at Mr. Goddard's at Leicester. He sat out with us for Worcester.

Got home in Safety and found all things well, and in Prosperity. Blessed be the Lord, who hath smiled on our going out, and returning home, who hath been our Shade upon our right hand, and preserved us and ours from all evil. To His Name be Glory from henceforth, and forever!

This journey consumed fifteen days. It surely was full of pleasure to our young couple,—but it was also full of dangers, hardships, and great weariness, which certainly appeal to us, who note the marvellous changes in the methods, and comforts of travel today.

In a journal of the same year we read: Town Meeting, the fourth time about the Meeting House, on repairing the old one, or dividing the Town, 23 Votes out of 47 for the first. Small Pox in Town, in several places.

Feb. 1739. Mr. Pennell here with Linen Cloth. Town Meeting, in part to see what to do about making more room in the Meeting House.

Mar. Town Meeting again upon the Article of the Meeting House, but still did nothing.

Apr. Powder Hill on Blaze, in a dry time, and an high wind and burnt me up all the fence upon the South East corner of my South Side.

Oct. Town Meeting to grant my Support. Unanimous for 200£.

Rode down to Lexington on Mr. S. Harrington's horse. Difficulty in finding the way from Weston. One Segar and one Mellage, my Pilots, it being Night. David Baverick and Sam Burupso bargained with me to clear my swamp, for 40 shillings per Acre, and their dinners while at work.

1740. A Fast was kept by this Church and Town on occasion of the Throat Distemper coming among us. Town Meeting for my support. Granted 120£ (without mention of wood) in case I supply the Pulpit this year.

June 1773. The Town met partly to see whether they would build a steeple (a number of persons having subscribed to give a Bell, and Clock if the Town would prepare for them) but it passed in the negative.

The Town met, again, to see whether it will be agreeable to them, to build a Steeple and have a Bell. Several persons have subscribed an hundred pound apiece. One (Mr. Seth Morse) 150£, Lieut. Baker 50 dollars, Capt. Maynard 100£—but it did not obtain. A great majority against it. The carpenters raised the West Porch at the Meeting House.

Of himself he writes: I am so near completing my 70th year that I have my thoughts running chiefly upon the words in Psalms 90:10—"The Days of our years are three-score years and ten, and if by reason of strength they be four-score years, yet is their strength, labour and sorrow; for it is soon cut off, and we fly away." Next Lord's Day, if I shall live to it, will be the last Sabbath of my 70th year. My mind is very closely exercised hereupon. May the Lord help me in preparing for it, both my sermons, and the frame of my spirit.

Sunday morning. I now desire most unfeignedly, and with all my best Powers to Bless the Lord that I am permitted to see the light of this morning, and to begin another year of Sabbaths. On this my Birth-Day, I bless God I have some sense of my situation in Life, but wish it was more impressive and effectual. May God graciously afford His Almighty influence!

A Town Meeting to see if the Town would not consent to some alterations to be made in the situation of the Pews, proposed to be built before the foreseats below, and to take away the great pew that is next to the Pulpit before, and above the Deacons' Seat. The former of these things the Town did nothing of; the latter was accomplished.

Oct. Blessed be God, who upholds me from one month to another. May I have Wisdom and Grace suitably to improve my Time, this rich Talent!

How swift my time flies! Another month gone. Lord make me to know mine end.

The Town had a meeting to sell their Remnants of Stuff and Stock. The carpenters and House joiners finish their work at the Meeting House. The

Painters and others are finishing the coloring and tarring over again the roof of the Meeting House.

A small number assist me at evening in drawing off the gravel, from the knoll behind my house. Several men from the Meeting House here. A good job was done. Their treat was Drink and Bread and Cheese

This being the last Lord's Day in our Ecclesiastical year, thanks were given to God for His grace, and long suffering in continuing us for the space of 49 years. A number of men with teams bring stones and level the ground and make what steps they can at the East end of the Meeting House.

Dec. Preached this morning on 2d Chron. 6:18, on occasion of so far completing and beautifying the Meeting House.

Ripley and Eaton from College, and going home as Invalids, came this way and drank Tea. They informed me that there is a great stir in Boston against landing the East India Company's Tea. Sent by Ripley to Mr. Stephen Salsbury, Huntington's Sermons.

Dec. 18. The world is filled with the news from Boston of the tumultuous rising and destroying many chests of Tea, sent by the East India Company. Mr. Mellen of Chauxit calls here. He confirms the shocking story of President Lock's awful fall! May I suitably improve this tremendous trial! Let him who thinks he stands take heed lest he fall.

I am asked to assist in a fast tomorrow at the House of Mr. Jacob Gibbs on the South of Southboro, on occasion of a great mortality of Throat Distemper. The said Gibbs having buried four of his children within a little while; a fifth ill and like to die May the Lord sanctify this awful visitation.

Dec. 25. I desire to give most hearty praise and thanks to God for the Birth of Jesus Christ, the great and only Saviour, though I don't know that this was the Day, nor do we publicly solemnize it as such. Thus closes the year O may I be prepared for the awful time when my life shall close.

Jan., 1774. How could I have imagined that so poor, weakly, and especially that so sinful and unworthy a creature would be spared to this Day! That I am indulged with another New Year's Day still! The Divine compassion, the Divine faithfulness and Truth do never fail. I desire with all my heart, with all my Powers, to bless and praise His glorious Name.

Feb. Returned from Mr. Gale's and found my son Alexander and his wife, with both their children, Robert Breck and Alexander, here.

Extremely difficult to get wood. The snow lately fallen & blown about into the Roads and paths rendering them very impassable to the wood Lots, but through Divine favor we have some supply at the door, which lasts yet.

21st. A number of persons came and got wood for me, at the Lot which is called Capt. Eph. Brigham's. Eight went to cut, viz.: Messrs. Nathan Townsend, Benjamin Fay Jr., Arthur Cary, Joseph Keenes, John Fay, Richard Temple, Tim Parker, Abel Tenny, and John (my son) joined them. The following numbers sledded, viz : Lieut. Baker with two teams, four oxen apiece; Barnabas Newton with four oxen; Capt. Benj. Fay's team, four Oxen, drove by his son Stephen; Dea. Wood sent a yoke of Oxen to join with mine, and Mr. Jona. Grout drove them. They all went twice, and Mr. Moses Nurse also brought one load; in all eleven Loads. At night the most of them supped here. May God reward them and bountifully, and grant me Grace to improve the Benefit.

22d. They that went for wood yesterday, so broke the Way, & made it fit to sled in; & the cutters cut so much more than was brought home, that Lieut. Baker in his generousness sent his team and man again today also to sled wood for me, and Mr. Newton in his goodness likewise, sent his team and man to sled up what was left and what another number of cutters cut, viz; Mr. Keene, John Fay hired, Stephen Maynard hired, Nathl. Chamberlin hired & Phinehas Brigham (son of widow Hitty). To the teams, add my own of three cattle & p. m. Dr. Hawes' steers instead of the mare, and my son John drove. Breck also procured Mr. Joseph Bond to come with his five cattle. They all went three times each—therefore twelve loads today.

24th. John Fay works for me from day to day in cutting wood in the Brigham lot—does today, and Elias a. m. sleds with our team—p. m. Dr. Hawes's steers and his young man to drive. Mr. Jos. Bond sleds today likewise. They brought in all today six loads.

These items must impress us with the effort it cost to live in those days and by comparison help us to appreciate our great blessings.

Oct. 22nd. In the morning we found the West window of the lower west room set up, wide open. Breck's desk open. The little front door open, with signs of violence in breaking it open: the lock broke off: three front drawers open, but nothing that we know of, as yet, missing: though the cupboard, where stood my silver cup, and in it a number of silver table spoons, also in another cup a number of silver tea spoons, was wide open.

It was doubtless a Thief who wanted Money, who entered the house, for no one of my family knows anything of the matter, and the window was no doubt fastened as usual; but a middle square of glass in the lower sash was taken out, and laid carefully away. From the hole, with one's arm, the stick which fastens down the window could be reached, and was taken away. God be praised no further damage was done; and may God grant Repentance to the Burglar!

Dec. 31st. Through the long suffering of God I am brought to the close of another year. The occurrences of it have been remarkable. Especially by the changes in the civil Government. Gov. Hutchinson gone to England. Gov Gage in his Room. The General Court is moved to Salem, which is made the chief seat of Government. The counsellors made by Mandamus. The company of cadets resign, and are disbanded. General Court soon dissolved. Boston Port blocked up by men of war; the common, the Neck, and Fort Hill will have five regiments. The Continental congress and the Provincial meet one at Philadelphia Sept. 5th,--the other, Concord and Cambridge. The Towns in confusion by reason that the Superior and Inferior Courts cease. Mobs & Riots, Whigs and Torys—as if our Happiness were nigh to an end! O God save us!

Feb., 1775. Town Meeting on many articles, viz.: whether we shall pay minute men, contribute to relief of Boston, etc.

21st. Town Meeting and Training. I went, and spoke to them on the head of their contributing to the relief of Boston, encouraging and exciting them to it. Willing to set an example myself, but apprizing them that since I knew of a number of poor people whom I should desire to communicate to, I might have the favor to be myself the distributor of my own alms. I earnestly commended their exerting themselves to obtain Military skill, Arms and Ammunition, &c,—to improve their time well, when they have Meetings and training—to endeavor after unity and harmony (for I perceived there were jars);—Exhorted to put away sin;—to be the true disciples of Christ, and do their utmost to prepare for the will of God concerning them. My mind and heart are filled with apprehensions of our Political state. May God Himself pity His People.

Our public state is more and more deplorable. Unless the God of Infinite Mercy and Power undertake for us, and change the hearts of men how can we escape the ruin which threatens?

Mar. 20th. Training of the Minute Men. People are variously tossed in their minds about the public state. We ride into Boston:—Viewed the King's Troops marching up School St., and went up to see their parade.

In the early morning of March 30th there was a noise of four Regiments marching out of Town under Earl Percy. Everybody was ignorant of the design; all were full of conjectures. The most imagined they were bound to Concord, to disperse the congress setting there, or to challenge the stores laid up in the Court House. But after a short space, the mystery was disclosed; they turned toward Dedham, and after about five miles march to Jamaica Plain they returned.

Apr. 8th. Mr. Nathan Fisher comes at eleven o'clock at night very much affrighted by what Dr. Hawes (who has come from the Provincial congress at Concord) relates to him of the public troubles.

19th. I rode over to Northboro expecting lecture,—but the world was full of alarms—the regulars ('twas said) had marched last night, and were gone to Concord—had killed six men at Lexington—posts were flying to rally the minute men everywhere. Our minute men under Capt. Edmund Brigham had marched. Capt. Seth Morse with his men marched. May the Lord of Hosts go with them and grant them salvation!

20th. The King's troops had been to Concord and did much mischief,—at the Magazine in special; to flour, ordnance, ammunition, houses (several set on fire); a number on both sides slain. But the regulars returned to Boston. A number of dead bodies chiefly of them scattered in the road. It is a day of so great trouble that it swallows up people's thoughts. Men are marching down toward Concord, amain. The news we have is very penetrating. At evening came Mr. Thomas Whitney, who had rid down as far as Charlestown. He has seen the sad effects of hot assaults and skirmishes. The account that the roads for a great way were strowed with dead men, is confirmed.

21st. In the morning Breck came home, having rid in the night. Relates that he met with difficulty in getting out of Boston; was stopped and searched three times; his sword and Pocket Pistol were taken away, but with much trouble, and going back into town and obtaining a permit from Collector Hamilton, they were restored. He went to Cambridge. Saw the great Multitudes that were gathering. He saw one buried without ceremony, and four more, who were slain there, were buried in one grave. Men are continually marching.

25th. Breck receives orders from the Captain at Cambridge to go to the Minute company.

26th. Breck leaves us to go to Cambridge.

28th. The last night was very restless to me, viewing the increase of our troubles. Boston close shut up, and the inhabitants in the utmost danger. Not a little concerned for my Son and brother.

An admirable company from New Haven under Captain Benedict Arnold, have marched down.

May. Letter to be delivered to Breck at Cambridge. He came home from Cambridge, arrived this morning about half past two: Relates another disaster, by the accidental going off of a Gun.

June. Breck returns from his journey to Cape Ann. Relates that our Provincials have taken 400 sheep from Deer Island,

Sunday while we were at exercise came the clerk of a large company of soldiers from Hartford, with compliments of Col. Geo. Pitkin, that I would go to Dea. Wood's and pray with them. In the morning he came again; the company being paraded before the Meeting House, I went and for convenience stood on the steps of the front door

News flies abroad that a Body of Regulars are gone over to Charlestown, and burned the Meeting House. An awful judgment of God upon us!

This journal here ends, July 24, 1775.

SARAH FAYERWEATHER GOULD.

May 3, 1906.

The Forbes Homestead.

My earliest memory goes back more than fifty years to a picturesque old house fronting on the country road from Westborough to Grafton. It is the oldest of three houses now grouped together on the old Forbes Homestead, although possibly not so old as the venerable elm tree so rent and broken by the ravages of time that its branches can hardly shelter its congenial neighbor with its long sloping roof and old fashioned "linter"

The front hall is nearly square and the narrow stairs, with their triple turns, lead from it to the chambers in the second story. On the right of the front door is the parlor, which used to be invaded only on extraordinary occasions The heavy timbers appear in the corners of this room, and of that across the hall, which used to be called the sitting room—each nearly 20 feet square. The center ceiling timber, a foot wide, has been enclosed with smooth boards in the parlor, but in the sitting room the bare oaken timber shows the beautiful wavy surface, made by a skillful workman more than 150 years ago.

These two front rooms enclose between them the immense chimney, which rests with its four flues, on a stone foundation about 10 feet square. Above the cellar the chimney is of brick and is finally so drawn together that it emerges from the garret but four feet square.

Back of these rooms, looking out upon a steep declivity, is the long narrow kitchen, which, with the little bedroom to the north, occupies the first story of the lean-to or "linter," as it is called in old deeds. At the northwest corner of this bedroom was an old Balm of Gilead tree, whose sticky but medicinal buds and tassels of flowers, succeeded by cotton enveloped seeds, were a constant delight. A row of Lombardy poplars helped sustain the cellar walls on this back side of the house. On either side of the front door were two lilac trees which constantly but unsuccessfully struggled to become bushes after the manner of lilacs, by sending up every spring and summer myriads of new red sprouts, which were ruthlessly cut down. Over the two large front rooms were originally two chambers of equal size, later divided by simple painted board partitions into four narrow chambers. The southeast chamber was occupied by my parents, and as far back as I can remember, my brother and I occupied a trundle-bed, which, each morning was pushed under the larger bed, there to remain until the very early evening hour, when it came rumbling forth to receive its small but tired tenants. We retired so early and the summer labor on the farm continued so late, that I remember being hastily called from my bed and dressed, so that I might aid my aged grandfather in bringing home the cows from Bentland pasture, more than a mile away. He was more than 80 years old and somewhat stiff. He drove a small bay horse in a large two-wheeled chaise, and excited my terror, at times, by following the cows grazing by the roadside over rocks and hummocks, so that he might reach them with his whip. I used to let down the bars, which were made light for a boy of five to handle, and occasionally had to hunt among the berry bushes for missing cows or chase them out of some orchard whose owner had left the bars down. The stairs leading to the bare unfinished attic passed an opening on the right which was a place for the deposit of newspapers and other rubbish. It was a dark mysterious cave leading back to the chimney and branching out in devious ways that I never dared to explore. I was never very much afraid of the dark but always breathed a sigh of relief when, after some errand to the garret, I had passed this opening in safety.

Back of the chambers in the second story was a garret under the sloping roof and a little chamber over the one to the north of the kitchen. In this little room was enacted weekly the family episode, usually accompanied by howls from us boys that the water was too hot, followed by the maternal assurance that it was not. An ell built on at three different periods extends from the kitchen southward $27\frac{1}{4}$ feet and for a width of 17 feet. In this was first a pantry, then a milk room, and next a wood room.

Within my memory the old brick ovens were used to bake the sixty Thanksgiving pies. The mince and puff paste crust were made according to a receipe which had come down in my mother's family from the time, before the Revolution, when an ancestor of hers received it from her English teacher of cooking in Boston.

When I was seven years old my father built the house now owned by Mr. N. M. Knowlton and the old house opposite was made into two tenements for the hired men.

In the south corner of the sitting room is a built-in cupboard, which with its hand carved work, emphasizes the fact that this house was much finer than most of the homes of the first settlers.

The driveway then as now led downward to the new barn south of the L of the house. A little farther back from the road and farther south was the oldest barn, the north end of which belonged to my father and the other to his father Dea Jonathan Forbes. The latter's barn yard extended from this oldest barn to the road and was bounded partly on the south by the upper barn and a shed. My grandfather moved out of the oldest house to that across the road now owned by Mr. Goddard in 1842, when my father was married and moved into the house I have described. It stood on land owned continuously by six generations of his ancestors from 1682, 35 years before Westborough became a town. The well is in front of the south end of the house. Its liquid contents were formerly extracted by a chain pump, as well as by a pump in the kitchen. The barnyard was supplied by running water from a spring in the Maynard lot to the south, through wooden logs now replaced by a lead pipe. The same aqueduct supplied the trough in my grandfather's barn-yard, which was separated from ours by a board fence. The south barn was moved by Rev. C. B. Kittredge across the road to the present site, back of the Goddard house, soon after he had bought the latter place from my aunt Eliza Sophia Forbes. Close to the roadside and just north of the barn-yard stood the old cider mill and carriage house owned in common by my father and grandfather, the former having the north end. Before my memory begins the ungodly cider mill had been removed. The only thing remaining that went around was the grindstone. The hired men delighted in seeing if they could bear on hard enough with their scythes to stop my turning the stone. Every autumn, with my fingers in my ears I watched the progress of a fat porker up the hill from the pen under the barn, to the old mill house where the hogshead of hot water received him, as soon as the village blacksmith had shown his skill in the ancient art of phlebotomy.

In the brief time allotted to me, I can but briefly sketch the history of this old house and of the land on which it stands. I have written a sketch of the Eaton Grant of which The Forbes Homestead was a part and this is printed in the History of Westborough. Theophilus Eaton was the first governor and the leading man in the New Haven Colony. Under his influence these early settlers in Connecticut in 1639 ignored King Charles I of England and the laws in force in the old country. Without recognizing their allegiance to any earthly sovereign they voted to adopt as their civil and criminal code the laws of Moses as given in the Old Testament, except the ceremonial part.

For more than forty years the colony of Massachusetts Bay owed Gov. Eaton and his heirs the £50 which was the consideration for the 500 acres granted to his heirs in 1680 and being the tract known later as the Fay Farm It received this name from the fact that the Brothers John and Samuel Fay actually built houses and lived on this tract while their uncles Thomas and John Brigham allowed their two-thirds to remain unimproved till many years later.

They purchased this grant from the Eaton heirs in 1682. Thomas Brigham took the central position of this grant for his share with some detached lots in the Assabet meadows and at the west end. He died Nov. 25, 1717, having deeded this tract, on which the three Forbes houses now stand, to his son Capt. Nathan Brigham of Marlborough. The latter conveyed this tract to his son Lieut. Nathan Brigham of Southborough and left a very interesting will, a copy of which I have with me. Capt. Brigham died Feb. 16, 1747.

He was for seven years selectman of Marlborough, the parent borough town, and held many places of honor and trust. He left his widow, among other liberal provisions, the sum of £20 for a mourning suit.

Lieut. Nathan Brigham, like his father and grandfather, never lived on this Eaton Grant but deeded it to his son Moses Brigham Feb. 7, 1754. No buildings or other improvements were mentioned in the deed. Moses was then 32 years old and was married to Mehetabel Grout five years earlier. She was the daughter of Lieut. Joseph Grout who was living on the John Brigham third of the Eaton Grant, on what is now known as the McTaggart farm.

Lieut. Brigham married Dinah Rice, sister of Silas and Timothy Rice, who were "captivated" by the Indians in 1704 and later became the leading chiefs of the Canadian Six Nations

For his second wife he married Elizabeth (Ward) Snow a widow with an unmarried daughter. His son Moses was not married until he was twenty-seven years old. The step-daughter had decided upon marrying him herself, when she learned that her step-brother's trips to the Eaton Grant were not for the sole purpose of clearing up a farm for his home, but to enjoy the fascinating society of the fair Mehetabel. Finally in a fit of jealousy she hamstrung his horse. Instead of keeping Moses for herself by this stratagem she drove him the earlier to Lieut. Grout's for a bride and to the new house still standing by the old elm. It is not probable that any house was built on this farm until about the time of his wedding in 1749. An aunt born in the old house told me more than forty years ago that it was then more than one hundred years old.

In 1728 that part of Sutton, now the home of the town poor, was annexed to Westborough. The first Dea. Jonathan Forbes. a son of the Scotch emigrant Daniel Forbes, lived here at that time. He owned several hundred acres in that vicinity including the grist and saw mill. His son, Rev. Eli Forbes, married Mary and Lucy, daughters of Rev. Ebenezer Parkman.

His son, Jonathan, also a deacon, bought a large part of the farm and died before his father, leaving a large family of children and a widow Joanna daughter of Dea. Simon Tainter, who lived on the adjoining farm. One of these children, Jonathan, also elected a deacon, married Sarah. daughter of Moses Brigham. The latter died in 1769 and all of the home farm except the widow's third was set off to his son Moses. This third Jonathan Forbes bought the farm from him in that year and for the next century it was owned by him and his descendants.

The inscription on his slate headstone in Memorial cemetery closes with these words.

"Afflictions sore long time I bore,
Physicians were in vain,
Till God did please with death to seize
And ease me of my pain."

He died June 3, 1805, and was succeeded as owner and occupant of the old house by Dea. Jonathan Forbes, his son who in turn was succeeded by his son Dea. Ephraim Trowbridge Forbes, the father of the writer of this sketch. Since his death in 1863, the house has been owned by his widow Catharine White Forbes and his son-in-law Chas. Brigham Kittredge. Mr. Kittredge, the oldest son of a former Westborough pastor, Rev. C.

B. Kittredge, married Catharine Salome Forbes of the eighth generation of Brighams and their Forbes descendants who continuously owned this estate. The present owner and occupant, George A. Ferguson, bought this place from Mr. Kittredge in 1871.

Additional Parkman Manuscripts.

In the library of the American Antiquarian Society in Worcester there are three bound volumes of the Diary of the Rev. Ebenezer Parkman. One of these is a book in which he wrote only on his birthdays. Of the other two books, the first covers the years from August 1, 1723, to Sept. 4, 1728. The other commences January 1, 1756 and closes May 31, 1761. These books were given to the Society in 1835 and were apparently the last things that were received by their brilliant young librarian, Christopher Columbus Baldwin, before his trip to Ohio which resulted in his death. We reach this conclusion because they are the last gifts recorded in the Gift Book in his hand writing.. Looking over this Book a few weeks ago we noticed that not only the Parkman Journal was given to the library at that time, but "very many manuscripts." These things were donated by Charles Breck Parkman of Westborough.

In one of the rooms of the Society, not open to the public we found two portfolios marked with the Parkman name, in which there have been kept safely for seventy years and more, about sixteen years of the Diary and other papers of great interest.

This newly discovered Diary covers the following periods of time;—

From January 1 1743 to January 15 1743
" January 1 1744 to January 22 1745
" January 23 1745 to December 31 1745
" January 1 1746 to December 31 1747
" January 1 1748 to December 31 1748
" January 1 1750 to January 23 1751
" January 24 1751 to January 31 1753
" January 1 1754 to December 31 1754
" June 14 1764 to June 30 1766
" July 1 1766 to December 31 1767
" January 12 1768 to July 3 1769
" November 10 1772 to November 21 1772
" July 24 1775 to August 31 1777

Besides these years of the Journal there were sermons upon more than one hundred and forty different texts, and on some texts they varied in length from a few pages to one, at least, of one hundred and fifty three pages; small pages, to be sure, but written in an extremely minute hand.

There was also a manuscript book, evidently prepared for the press, called "Memoirs of Mrs. Pierpont." Mrs. Pierpont was the wife of Rev. James Pierpont of New Haven and seems to have been a very intimate friend of the Parkmans. In fact in the Diary for 1746 we find this entry on the anniversary of the marriage of Mr. Parkman to Hannah Breck;—"But how ardent and united were we this day nine years ago! when our nuptials were celebrated at Mr. Pierpont's in Boston."

There are also a number of papers of his college days, a few family letters, some books of manuscript poems, etc., which he had copied, and other less important papers.

It would seem that one of these portfolios, containing only sermons, was given to the Society by Rev. Francis

Parkman of Boston. Certainly some of the sermons were received from him.

This newly discovered Diary, like that we have known so long is rich in local historical material and quaint and interesting pictures of the day.

Among other things we have the date when Stephen Maynard's house was finished; "February 1 1765, I dined at Capt. Maynard's. The carpenters finish there." May 15 1766 "I went to the raising of Lieut. Forbush's house and was at the entertainment."

A very few extracts from this rich mine must be sufficient for today.

In 1745 Mr. Parkman speaks of the death of two children of a Mrs. Billings and adds "They were buryed by the new Meeting House. The first that have been buried in that place."

A few days later, still another child died in this family and he writes;--"Sept. 16, 1745, a story has got about of a dream of Mrs. Billings and which I took the freedom to inquire into and which she confirmed, viz that she saw a man bring the coffin of her youngest child into the house, upon which she took on, but presently there came in another man with a *large* coffin and said to her that she had not need to take on for her *child*, for here was a coffin for her also, for *she* should die next.

N. B. Mr. Hale who lives near the new burying place ('tis said) saw a large coffin as well as a small one in the air just over the burying place last Tuesday evening immediately after the burying of Mr. Billings his children, which stories much fright people about Mrs. Billings' death."

The cemetery thus referred to in September 1745 cannot be Memorial Cemetery, for Mr. Parkman knew the burial place of his flock from the time of his arrival in Westborough in 1724 for more than half a century. His first wife, Mary Champney, the mother of his five oldest children, died Jan. 29, 1735 and a modest headstone still marks her grave in our oldest cemetery. In the great Book of Records of the Proprietors of Marlborough on page 294 we find this entry—"At a meeting of the Proprietors held at the Meeting honse in Marlborough 2nd Monday in January 1727-8, Set apart 1¼ acre of land in Westborough, where the inhabitants always have buried their dead on the westerly side of the road leading to Sutton to be for a burying place for ever."

In book 2nd, page 177 is a record of 147 rods of land laid out to Westborough South Precinct. I hold in my hand the original layout.

In Book 1 at page 297 is a record of three acres granted to Westborough for a burying place, and this is supposed to be the old neglected and abandoned town cemetery in Northborough on the north side of the road leading easterly from the road to Westborough and being the first road to the east after crossing the boundary bridge over the Assabet River. I have a plan of this diamond shaped cemetery received from Mrs. Geo. C. Davis of Northborough, whose husband owned land on three sides of it. The old headstones are either prostrate or buried in the forest which now covers these graves of the pioneers of that part of the larger Westborough.

November 30, 1750 Mr. Parkman made the following interesting entry: "Billy as he was cutting wood at the door cut his ancle. The wound was somewhat crosswise and bled very much. It was in the forenoon when his brothers which were able to do anything were gone from home: Ebenezer to work for Mr Rogers and Thomas to Mr Goddard's Mill. (Thomas was then

21 years old and Billy 10 yrs) We tried Puff Ball to stop the bleeding but to no purpose. After some time the blood running fresh still, we took off the bindings and filled the sore with sugar but neither did this succeed. We sent about noon for Mrs. Hepsibah Maynard, both the Captain and his wife came. It seemed to be stanched for a time but flowed again. He had now bled so much that we were concerned at the event. Thomas was groaning at the toothache and wanted to go to Dr. Smith to get his tooth drawn out. I therefore hastened him although it was evening to bring the Dr. to Billy. We had also tried the scraping of tanned leather and scorched cotton and still fresh puddles appeared. N. B. Several times when it was opened the blood spurted out as in phlebotomy. While Tommy was gone and tarried long, our fears arose high, for Billy had lost so great a Quantity of Blood that he began to turn pale and we did not know but that it was still running. I ardently committed him and his case to God who is a perfect help in time of trouble. After a while the Blood ceased as we conceived nor did any more appear throughout the night. Blessed be God for his sparing Mercy! Thomas did not come till past nine o'clock and no doctor with him, but got his own tooth out; or rather a part of it, for it broke in the jaw. Molly is also in great anguish with toothache so with my own lameness we have no small trouble in the house. But I humbly wait on God. My wife watched with Billy."

Three years and nine months of Mr. Parkman's Diary are now in the collections of the Mass. Historical Society, Boston. Two years and six months belonging to Mrs Edward Tuckerman of Amherst, Mass. have been printed by the Westborough Historical Society. Ten years and six months are bound up in the library of the American Antiquarian Society, Worcester, Mass Sixteen years, unbound, are in the same library. Six years and three months are in the possession of Mrs Sarah Fayerweather Gould. Possibly other volumes of this Diary are in existence.

Westborough is fortunate above most country towns in having the chronicles of its early life and of the daily thoughts and doings of its early inhabitants preserved in such interesting fashion by its best informed and most graphic penman for at least thirty-nine years and four months.

WILLIAM T. FORBES.
Worcester, June 16, 1906.

The Thomas Forbush House.

The subject of this sketch is the ancient house which formerly stood in a field, or large lot, far back from the junction of Lyman and East Main streets. The avenue which led up from Main street to the house is now marked by a row of large trees.

Years and years ago, Daniel Forbush, born in 1620, left his home in Scotland and came to America. In 1660 he married Rebecca Perriman of Cambridge. Thomas was born in 1667, being the second son, and brother of Samuel, whose house was the subject of the March calendar. We find his name among the signers of a petition in 1702 for a new town to be set off from the old town of Marlboro. The tract asked for included not only the present territory of Westboro and Northboro but the whole of Shrewsbury, a large part of Boylston and a wide strip of the northern section of Grafton. There was much litigation concerning boundaries and ownership. The petition was not granted and the village of Chauncy remained a part of Marlboro for 15 years longer.

Thomas Forbush's name appears in Rev. Mr. Parkman's diary as one of the 27 "first families" of the town. In those early and struggling days there was the same pride of blood and priority that obtains today.

Thomas Forbush was one of the 12 men beside the minister to form the new church in October, 1724. No woman's name appeared until the following July, when six women were received. Evidently there were no sewing circles or church suppers in those "good old days." We find Thomas standing up in meeting opposing the minister, whom he accused of not falling in with the vote of the town on some important matter. Whereupon the minister arose and laid down the law and right in such a masterful way that "there was peace for 40 years."

Thomas Forbush married Dorcas Rice and set up housekeeping in the house we are considering. We are all familiar with its exterior appearance. There were two rooms front, one each side of the seldom used front door; back of these, extending nearly the entire length of the house from east to west, was the kitchen. A very small room was partitioned off from one end, which was used as a cheese room, a very important place for the making and curing of this most valuable and edible product of the farm. Doubtless the sleeping apartment was in one corner of the big kitchen, being well warmed and lighted by the fire in the wide and deep fire place. What better or more comfortable place in which to sleep when there was drifting snow and howling winds without?

"What matter how the night behaved?
What matter how the north wind raved?
Blow high, blow low, not all its snow
Could quench our hearth fire's ruddy glow."

Perhaps the bride of today would consider it not quite up to her requirements for a dainty boudoir, but there was much in that primitive life to bring out all that was heroic in man and woman. Here the children were born, grew to manhood and womanhood. Mr. Parkman writes in his diary August 21, 1726: "I went down to Thomas Forbush's, and was intending to marry his dauter Eunice to Mr. Cornelius Cook, but they could produce me no legal certificate &c." He adds, the next day: "I again rode to Mr. Forbush's and married Cornelius Cook to Eunice Forbush (so they will spell their name.)" Aug. 18, 1728, he records, in speaking of the death of Mrs. Lieut. Forbush: "A very meek, patient. Godly person under her sufferings, she bore them many years of her life by sickness & suffering."

Thomas' second son was born in 1695; married Hannah Bellows in 1719. He filled many offices of trust, from 1727 to 1755, was selectman; from 1728 to 1751, town clerk. Thomas and Hannah had 13 children. Thomas deeded to his son Thomas (grandson of the first Thomas) for $120, 35 acres in Chauncy Plain with two dwelling houses and a barn. One of these houses still stands on the west corner of Lyman and East Main streets, afterwards owned by Cornelius Cook, who had married Eunice Forbush. This house was known as the Cook house and afterwards was the property of Dr. James Hawes and known as the Hawes' place.

Ebenezer, seventh son of Thomas and Hannah, born in 1731, bought of his father in 1765, 200 acres of land; lived for some time in the house with his father, and was later administrator of the estate.

In 1783 Ebenezer sold 100 acres to Thomas Andrews, who had married his eldest daughter Hannah in 1776, so as to contain one-half of the 200 acres he had bought of his father Thomas, with one-half of the dwelling house and barn and out houses to be equally divided between them. In 1790 Ebenezer sold his half to his son-in-law, Thomas Andrews. In 1813 he sold to his second son, Elliot Andrews, 23 acres of the home farm, with buildings, reserving the west end of the house.

In 1816 Thos. Elliot Andrews sold 27 rods at southwest corner of the lot to the First Baptist society for stables or sheds for the use of the attendants of the Baptist church, which was built that year on the west side of Lyman street between the Hawes house and the corner. The land was mortgaged in 1825 to Daniel Waldo and in 1826 to Caleb W. Forbush; in 1829 Onslow Peters acquired the equity of redeeming the part on the north side of the great road, and in 1831 all these parties relinquished their rights in the land to Nehemiah Carter.

In 1842 the latter conveyed 12½ acres with buildings, which covered the site of the old house, to Merrick R. Stevens, and he the same in 1845 to Emeline Abigail Bailey, wife of Sam'l. R. Bailey. In 1882 Samuel K. Bailey, son of the last named, who had the right by inheritance from his mother, conveyed the same to Elizabeth S. Bailey of Milton, in whose name the land was assessed in 1905.

This house, called the Thomas Forbush house, must have been one of the oldest in town. There are three families, or some members of these families, still living here who have resided in the old house. Mr. Solomon Taylor Fay lived there before he built his house on the adjoining lot on East Main street. Mr. Fay was guardian of the minor children of Thomas Elliot Andrews Mrs. Brittan, mother of John W. Brittan, lived there in 1852, from whom many facts concerning the house have been received. The last family to live there was Mr. Patrick Haley.

In early times every able bodied man was obliged to belong to the militia. This estate on the corner was the favorite meeting place for drill and the annual muster was held there when good cheer abounded much in the form of hard cider and New England rum. With a little help of the imagination one can see, as he passes by on the trolley cars, the companies forming, the strut of the drum major, and hear the command, right face—forward march.

The old house with all its sweet and sad memories of birth, marriage and death is in ashes, having been burned June 29, 1895.

ABBY K. HARVEY.

July, 1906.

The First Davis House.

"Built in 1707 to 1711—remodelled in 1881," is the record that Mr. Broaders wrote on the stringer of the stairs in cellar way. If correct, it would make this one of the oldest houses in town. The earliest reference to it we have at hand in any deed is that of Oct. 11, 1739, when John Chamberlin deeded it to Seth Rice. It stood near the Tomblin Bridge over the Assabet. The land comprised eight and one half acres, bounded on the north and east "by highway as it now goeth .. with dwelling house and fences and everything standing and lying thereon."

In 1754, Seth Rice, who had served as Town Treasurer for four years some while before, sold the property to Phinehas Maynard, his son-in-law, who had just before married his daughter, Dorothy Rice.

In 1763, it passed back to Mr. Rice, who sold it with additional land on the west side of the river to Mr. Maynard, In the county road book of 1765, it is marked as the dwelling of Jonathan Hero.

It was while in Mr. Maynard's possession, we judge, that Isaac Davis lived there. In 1772 he had married Anne Brigham, the stepdaughter of Stephen Maynard and whose mother was the niece of Mrs. Parkman. They soon after occupied this house and together united with the church in 1773. Mr. Davis was a tanner whom Capt. Maynard sought to teach his trade to his son Antipas, hoping thereby to cure the lad of his disposition to wander from home. But the plan did not work. Antipas made his home with the Davis family, but one evening at Mrs. Forbes tells us in "The Hundredth Town," he started forth with his belongings and was not heard from for twelve years.

Isaac Davis and wife had several distinguished sons of whom the elder ones were born in this house, but John, afterwards the Governor of the State, was born in the house bought by his father in 1781 originally built by Dea. Tomblin on the North side of the river.

The pastor, Mr. Parkman, often called at the first house, once in 1779, writing on his return from Shrewsbury "I stopt at Mr. Isaac Davis, about soal leather"

"Isaac Davis," Mrs. Forbes writes, "is today remembered as 'large, tall and stern;' one of the representative men of his time. He outlived Anne Brigham by many years, and was twice married after her death." It was the joint ownership which the second wife had with a former neighbor in a barrel churn, that led to the dispute, which Mr. Davis put an end to by sawing the churn in halves.

Later he was prominent in his official relation as deacon in settling the difficulties that arose under the rather arbitrary ministration of Pastor Whitney of the North Church.

It was this same good deacon of whom

the story is told that he checked his grandson's delight, on the way to church, in the pranks of a squirrel, by "a sharp twist of the ear and the quick reproof that 'squirrels are not to be mentioned today,'"

I find no mention of Mr. Davis' ownership of this house and he was probably tenant only of Phinehas Maynard, for in 1784, Daniel Steward and wife Dorothy, and in 1792, Calvin Rice and wife Betty (the wives being daughters and heirs of Mr. Maynard) sold their rights to Beriah Ware. In 1800 Calvin Rice and wife sold to Phineas and Joseph Davis, sons of Isaac, one half of twenty-two acres and the latter sold the same to Beriah Ware.

The latter, in 1804, deeded fifteen acres with all buildings to Amasa Maynard. He lived in what is now known as the Wayside Cottage of the Lyman School. This tract passed in 1805 to Fortunatus Nichols, who two years later sold it with other land back to Mr. Maynard

In 1812, the latter sold to Jacob Broaders, cordwainer, the sixteen acres on which the house before us stood.

This Mr. Broaders was the son of the old Jacob Broaders referred to in the Parkman Diary, but I find no evidence of his having owned the place. His estate was appraised in 1786 and did not include this. He may have lived here, as well as his son, Jacob Jr., for some time before he bought it.

Mr. John Cobb of Malden, whose memory reaches back to the Broaders family who were his neighbors across the way in his young days, speaks of them in a kindly way. He recalls many boyish pastimes in which he took part with them.

"Mr. J. Broaders," he writes, "was a small farmer and besides a custom shoemaker. He followed his trade when work was finished on the farm. He was a thorough workman. His only son, Hiram, when he was old enough, taught school and in after years when his father was getting aged attended to the farm exclusively.

The elder Broaders was a great reader and wiled away much leisure time reading the Egyptian hieroglyphics tilted back in his old kitchen chair. His greatest pastime seemed to be fishing on the Assabet stream. He was acquainted with all the spots which the fish inhabited and he often trailed for pickerel and good luck always followed him."

It is a pleasure to read of the good services that Mr. Cobb, at much sacrifice, was able to render his old friends, especially when bereavement befell them, and the mother and father were called to their rest in 1847.

The homestead of forty acres was left by the father to his son Hiram Lee Broaders, who always lived on the "Haven of Rest" farm as he was wont to call it. He died in 1896 aged 77 years. His administrator sold the property in 1897 to George H. Johnson, the present owner.

It is very difficult to get any full description of the old house as it was in the early days. It was two stories in front with the long sloping roof in the rear, and was in the early times painted red. It occupied the same space that the main part of the present house now does. The rather deep cellar is under three-fourths of it, the other fourth being taken up with the stone foundation of the old chimney.

In the four rooms in the first story as in those in the second story, the corner beams and in most of the rooms the large cross beams in the ceilings are in plain evidence today. These and the floor beams are seemingly sound and good for another century. Several of the floors are still laid with the old hard wood boards, often eighteen inches in width.

Owing to the short time that this delayed sketch has been in our hands, much in it will be found imperfect. but any corrections or additions to it will be welcomed.

S. INGERSOLL BRIANT.
August, 1906.

The Gershom Brigham House.

The Thomas Brigham of Marlborough, who bought, in 1682, the central portion of the Eaton farm and who willed the East part of this to his son Nathan, which was later the Forbes' homestead, bestowed sundry pieces of the West part of the farm to his sons, David and Gershom, October 8, 1733. David assigned his interest in these to his brother Gershom of Marlborough, a physician.

These lands, doubtless, included the site of the old house before us. This Dr. Gershom Brigham conveyed in 1741 certain pieces of land to his son, Gershom, among which were 80 acres formerly a part of Sutton as it stood divided to him and his brother Nathan. The first mention that we have of the dwelling house is in a deed of May 26, 1743, of land "West and Southwest of where Gershom Brigham now dwelleth."

This Gershom Brigham, on November 16, 1779, deeded to Dr. Gershom, his son, of Fitzwilliam, N. H., certain lands and also "the East half of the upright part of the dwelling house of the said Gershom Brigham with privileges in the cellar & well—also of laying in wood by the house through my land & of passing & repassing from the causeway &c,"

On January 31, 1783, an additional deed from Gershom Brigham to his son, Dr. Gershom, runs thus: "To encourage him to settle with me & in consideration of an obligation which my said son has this day entered into for the payment of certain sums of money to his sister Mary &c, I grant to him one undivided moity or one half part of my land in Westboro &c, also one undivided half of the kitchen part of my dwelling house & one half of the barn on premises."

February 7, 1799, this land with all his other in Westborough passed to his sons, Silas and Timothy, together with Gershom, who are to take care of the father as he stands in need, with certain exceptions in favor of their sister Mary.

The will of this Doctor Gershom Brigham, dated July 16, 1810, "touching such worldly estate as God in his Providence has lent unto me" after gifts to his widow and other children, leaves to his son Josiah all real and personal estate. In a codicil to this, dated August 21, 1810, he gives to his sons, Benjamin and Joseph, a certain sum as compensation "for money & labour which they advanced for building a house which I consider their full share of said house." This may refer to the house on the West side of the road, opposite the old house, which is reputed to have been built shortly before 1810.

The estate was, on October 9, 1871, sold to Azubah, the widow of Joseph, and through her executors, on February 1, 1890, passed to Walter F. Nichols, the present owner.

Thomas Brigham came to America in 1635. His son Thomas was born in 1641, and married Mary Rice. They had three sons, Nathan, David and Gershom (the latter born in 1680, who was a doctor and surveyor) and a daughter Mary. This Gershom had a son Gershom born in 1712, who had a son Gershom born about 1746, who was a doctor. He had a son Josiah and twins, Joseph and Benjamin, born in 1780, who married Hannah and Lucy Hardy.

The following entries in the diary of that man of God, Rev. Ebenezer Parkman. A. M., regarding Dr. Gershom Brigham and family will be of interest here, the first being in the very severe winter of 1779-80, under date of Dec. 27: "Called at Mr. Gershom Brigham's and began to take Thomas' Spy of him.

Jan. 22, 1780. Elias goes on Racketts to Dr. Gershom Brigham's. A newspaper of Dec. 30 is ye Last.

June 2. Dr. Gershom Brigham makes me a visit respecting ye Baptism of his new born twins.

Aug. 3. Visit Mr. Gershom Brigham's wife, who languishes.

Aug. 28. On Deac. Wood's Horse I rode to Mr. Gershom Brigham's to see his Wife, who is dangerously ill. The state of her Soul deplorable as well as her Body. She was very sorry yt she had neglected ye Lord's Supper. She was in much Confusion. I prayed with her and ye Family. I dined there.

Aug. 31. Mr. Gershom Brigham brings his Wife's Earnest Desire yt I would visit her again & preach a Sermon there today. I complied—delivered a short Discourse (as I could) from several passages in Isa. 55. 'Hear and your Soul shall live.' May God bless what was delivered. Mrs. Br. is brot very low.

Sept. 5. Mr. Gleason came and informed yt Mr. Gershom Brigham's Wife dyed this morning and ye Survivors desire me to attend ye Funeral next Thursday.

Sept. 7. I rode one of Alexander's Horses to ye Funeral of Mrs. Brigham (wife of Mr. Gershom) & prayed there."

Thanks are due our worthy President, Rev. S. I. Briant, for the material provided for this article and to Mrs. Esther M. Howell, who wrote the following tribute to the memory of Col. Josiah Brigham:

Col. Josiah Brigham, a lifelong friend of my father, was purely a son of the soil—a typical New Englander, with traits of character which the present generation would do well to emulate. Sturdy in principle as well as physique; affable, genial, approachable by friends, but keenly discriminating between friends and so-called friends. Quick to respond to a call for assistance from a worthy source, generous where generosity was a blessing to the recipient, trustful even though it robbed him of valued friendship, honorable to a degree approaching the Master's ideal and the example He set for His following. Warm hearted, sympathetic, and allied with all that made for peace, harmony and good will—misunderstood, misjudged and misplaced in his local environment, he lived on in the shadows which enveloped him, in the full belief that at some future day, all would be made clear and the inharmonious harmonized to a sweet and tender symphony—the bitternesses would be sweetened and all that marred the beauty of the life-canvass be eliminated, unfolding a newer and fresher delineation of the old theme. With little penchant for public service, his honors in that line were few, spiritual to a degree little dreamed by his average acquaintance, his communings with himself and God were frequent and prolonged, and could his heart have been lain open to the public gaze and perusal a most astounding revelation would have been the result, for he was far in advance of the thinkers and tenets of his time.

And thus among his old compeers and associates, he passed the full quota of his years, read in many languages by as many people, yet wholly unread in the true vernacular, i. e., misunderstood to the last. None *knew* him save those few to whom his heart had pledged unswerving allegiance and from whom he had received the same blessed assurance. He was but one of many so misjudged, but for sake of truth and a desire for justice we gladly pen this simple tribute to one who was so endeared to our paternal ancestor."

This house built more than 163 years ago and which has witnessed the coming and passing of so many generations with the dangers, hardships and privations of the earlier years and the increased comforts and enjoyments of the later times, still stands in a good state of preservation. It has continued to be occupied until recently as a dwelling.

The good old minister who preached as *short* a sermon as he could to lighten the path through the dark valley for the dying wife of Dr. Gershom Brigham at her home, was laid to rest in Memorial cemetery 124 years ago, but the house may stand for many years to come as one of the interesting landmarks of the olden time.

A. FRANKLIN BROWN.

September, 1906.

The Haskell House.

This house, one of the oldest in town, stands upon high ground in the east part of the town, on the old road to Boston, at the corner of East Main and Haskell streets. It is about two miles from the village. Like many other old houses, it had two large rooms on each floor with an entry between. There was a large chimney in the center with separate flues for each fireplace and a large fireplace in the kitchen back of the front rooms, with a small room at the end used as a bedroom or a milk room. There was a large brick oven. Also, a room back of the kitchen led into the shed. A few years since the old chimney was removed and many improvements made.

As early as 1756, the site of the house "with all the natural property thereto belonging" was sold by Timothy Warrin to Thomas Chase. The latter may have built the house soon after this, for in 1759 he sold the land "with the dwelling house on same" to Benoni Chase of Sutton. Two years later John Beaton, blacksmith, bought it, and in 1764 sold it, with the house and also a blacksmith shop on it, to Phinehas Haskell. The latter disposed of a half interest in the estate to his son Asa in 1792, and it remained in his hands and those of his descendants till 1901 Additional acres were added to it from time to time. A plot of the land by Nahum Fisher in 1842 included 37¼ acres.

In 1902 it was owned by Mrs. Maria C. Chase, and in 1903 it passed to the present owner, Mrs. Grace M. Fields.

In 1632 William Haskell, one of the three brothers who came from England, settled in Gloucester, Mass. He was the father of Joseph Haskell, whose son Ebenezer was the father of Phinehas

Phinehas Haskell was born in 1732. He married Susanna Burnam in 1761. About this time he came to Westborough and bought what is now called the Haskell place. He was a farmer and tilled the soil for a livelihood; also a blacksmith. The shop stood between the house and where the schoolhouse now stands. He was puritanic in his principles. To *do* right and to *be* right was his great aim in life, He was a decided man and firm in what he considered right and just. So far as we can learn, he did not officially take part in the business of the town. He was a home man, looking after the interests of his family, and laboring to improve his land, setting out trees, etc. There has been very nice fruit on the place and berries, which the children enjoyed.

He did not make a profession of religion until he was 80 years old. About this time Rev. Jonathan Edwards passed through town and preached in Framingham. Mr. Haskell went to hear him. He became interested and openly professed his faith. He, with his grandson Elijah, aged 17, were baptised in a small stream of water near Dea. Beeman's house (since burned) on Flanders road. The Deacon prepared the upper part of his house for Baptist meetings. They also had frequent meetings at the Haskell house, before the first Baptist church was built.

Mr. Haskell had a family of six children, five sons and one daughter. Caleb, the oldest living child, was born in 1764. He studied medicine and in 1793 he was a practising physician in Hampton Falls He was never married. I have a letter from him written at that time, dated, "Hon'd Father, July 3d, 1793," and closes, "My love to Marm and brothers and sisters." (This was what mothers were called at that time). He died Aug. 17, 1817, aged 53. His daughter Susanna married Mr. Seth Grout of Northborough. Her daughters, Susan and Eliza, both married Holbrooks. Her oldest married Daniel Holbrook, Some will remember Holbrook's store, at the corner of Main and South streets where Mr. Gates' store now stands. The old building was removed. After Mr. Holbrook's death Mrs. Holbrook married Mr. Cyrus Gale, Sr., of Northborough. On leaving Westborough for her new home, she kindly donated her house on South street, the Bates' place, to the Baptist church for a parsonage. Eliza married Levi Holbrook, whose son Levi is a business man in New York City.

Mr. Haskell spent some of his last days in Northborough with his daughter. He died suddenly at his old home in Westborough, aged 82 years, and was buried in the northwest part of Memorial cemetery.

His son Phinehas Haskell, Jr., went to Maine about 1810. He had three daughters and one son. The two oldest daughters married Longfellows, brothers. They settled in Machias, Me. The youngest was a cripple. Some of our oldest residents may remember Lucy Haskell, who often visited Westborough. stopped with Mrs. Holbrook and other relatives,—a good old lady, walking on crutches. His son Phinehas married and settled in Feltonville, now Hudson, where some of his descendants now live.

His son Asa Haskell was born in 1765, was married to Lydia Wheelock, daughter of Col. Moses Wheelock, colonel in the revolutionary war. He also died in this house, aged 63, and was buried in the Memorial cemetery. Any one walking down Main street can read his epitaph. It was said of him that after his return from the war he never complained of food or comforts, for he suffered much in the war. Those old veterans did not have the comforts and care that those who were in our late war enjoyed. The chair that he died in and the knife and fork that he carried with him through the war are still preserved.

Mr. Asa Haskell married Lydia Wheelock in 1793 and brought her to his home. They were blessed with five children, two sons and three daughters. They all lived to a good old age: Lydia 76, Clarinda 88, Elijah 90, Asa 91, Mary 94. In 1803 the family were all sick with fever; his mother also, at Northborough. Mr. Haskell, caring for them all, took the fever and could not rally. He died a young man, 38 years old,—a sad loss to the wife and mother with five little children around her.

Mr. Haskell was a good Christian man. He had a license to preach and was soon to be ordained. He often went to the surrounding towns to do good and improve his talent as the door opened. His word was to be depended upon; a very conscientious man. Perhaps some might say to a fault. One instance: A meeting was held at a Mrs. Clark's, who lived nearly three miles from his home, near where Mrs. Reuben Boynton now lives The house is not there today. On leaving, Mrs. Clark said to him, "Will you empty a pail of water, as you pass out?" It was a very cold night. He says, "I will." It did not come to his mind again until he had retired. He told his wife he must go and do it. She tried to persuade him not to go, but he said, "I must. I promised to." He got up and took another six mile walk in the cold. He could keep his word, and he did. In 1796, May 21, he, with Mr. James Hawes, Jr., my two grandfathers, were the first baptised by immersion in Westborough, at Lake Chancey, or Chancey Pond, as it was called then. They united with the church in Sutton, before a Baptist church was organized in town.

But to return to the widow and the five fatherless children. She looked for divine help and obtained it. She was advised by friends to put her older children out, "bind them out," as it was called at that time, until they were 18 or 21. But she said "No," she should keep them together as long as she could. She kept cows, selling butter and cheese, and sheep, spinning and weaving the cloth to make the children's clothes. By hard work and economy she accomplished it, still keeping her doors open to the traveling preachers to rest and hold meetings, inviting in her neighbors. She brought her children up in the fear and admonition of the Lord, to work and do what they could, giving them what education she was able to, teaching them to love the Bible and to keep the Sabbath holy. One Sunday one of her little boys wandered down to the woods, not far from the house. (They were not allowed to go on Sunday). Just as he came to the woods two large dogs came out upon him. He thought of the two bears his mother had read to him about in the Bible. He was much frightened, ran to the house, and never ventured out again on Sunday.

Years passed. Two young ministers came to the house, just commencing their life work. They saw the two eldest daughters, just coming into womanhood, in the bloom of youth and activity, intelligent, for they had improved their privileges. The mother was then willing to give her daughters away, as much as she loved them, to help those devoted men in gathering in sheaves for the Master. They soon took them to New York State, which was then called "out west," for it took them a week to go and a week to return; no public conveyance as now. But they did not forget Mother. They often visited the old home, and many interesting spiritual letters are still preserved. They wrote often, if postage was 18¾ cents a letter. I have a full sheet from one written just before her 94th birthday. They lived to a good old age and proved to be excellent wives and mothers, helpers in their husbands' work, both spiritual and temporal. Revivals followed wherever they went. All died in peace, feeling their life work was done.

One incident in the life of this grandmother, that we all loved so well, was her great disappointment, as she called it. In 1780, the 19th of May, the dark day as it was called, her father, Col. Wheelock, lived at that time, a short distance above the Bartlett place. They were going to have a nice dinner that she loved. It being so dark they did not prepare the dinner. Her father coming home at night from town could find his way only by holding on to the fence. She was so disappointed that she always remembered it. She was then but nine years old. She died in 1855, aged 82 years.

In 1822 Elijah Haskell was married to Mary L. Hawes, daughter of James Hawes, Jr. He also took his wife to his home. Two little girls here first saw the light of day; both now living, over 80 years old; Mrs. Emily A. Child and the writer of this. Mr. Haskell lived in this house after marriage six years; then went to his wife's old home, the Hawes place. Lydia, the youngest daughter, remained at home to care for mother, and was a great comfort to her.

Asa Haskell, Jr., the youngest child, born in 1803, lived at home until he was 21. On hearing of the great excitement in the western states and that many families were moving from New England and New York toward that vast country, he caught the fever and desired to see for himself. In 1825, he wrote home a very interesting letter describing his travels, the country as it was at that time, etc. His letter was published in the Chronotype a few years ago. But he decided to return to the old home and cultivate New England soil. He married in 1836, Achsah Warren, Dea. Abner Warren's daughter. The house was repaired, two rooms being added. It was painted and other improvements were made. A new barn was built later. He followed in the steps of his father and took his wife to the old homestead. Seven children were born to them, five sons and two daughters. Three sons enlisted in the army. One never returned. He was wounded in "Deep Run" battle Aug. 15, 1864, and died in the hospital near Philadelphia, Aug. 29. Later his grave was found by a cousin and a small tree was planted there. Two sons married and left town. Many remember the sad time when the remaining three, Mary, Sarah and Fred, who lived so happily together, passed away so suddenly to the great beyond, within two weeks, leaving the house without an occupant. Their parents had died some years before.

No one of the remaining family caring to live there, the house was sold and passed out of the Haskell name, having been in possession of the Haskell family nearly 140 years. There have been 20 births and 13 deaths in this home, perhaps more.

One of the seventh generation,

LYDIA MARIA BRITTAN.

October 31, 1906.

The Gale Tavern.

As early as Jan. 21, 1717, (the year when Westborough was incorporated) we find that Isaac Amsden, Sr., sold to his son Isaac, "30 acres of upland where the said Isaac Amsden's house now stands." This, we suppose, was the house before us. On Jan. 29, 1722, this Isaac Amsden, Jr., "in consideration of a fartherly Love & Will which I do Bear my Son Jacob Amsden," conveyed to the latter a tract of 60 acres, "all of which is one intire piece which has only a highway through same by the said Jacob Amsden's dwelling house."

Other lands were added to the estate, 16¼ acres in 1738 from Samuel Brigham, and 5¼ acres from Eleazar Beaman. These 22 acres Jacob Amsden sold in 1749 to Isaac Amsden, a nephew, who then conveyed the same, with the "North East end of the dwelling house, that is to say, half the said house at the North East end of same and at the chimney," to Thaddeus Gale, blacksmith, and Abijah Gale, yeoman. These two brothers had married Mr. Amsden's cousins, Lydia and Abigail, daughters of Jacob Amsden.

In 1752 Thaddeus Gale sold his title to his brother Abijah, and in the following June, Jacob Amsden conveyed his rights to a piece of 20 rods, bounded "West through house in which said Jacob do now dwell to an apple tree & the West half of dwelling house with half of the cellar under the other half." In the partition of the estate of Jacob Amsden in 1766, among other lands, the lot with the house fell to the daughter, Abigail Gale.

The house itself was probably built with the long sloping roof at the back side but it was virtually two stories in the main part having three back rooms and a room in the ell in the second story in addition to the two front rooms as they are now. There was a one story ell extending back with large kitchen and woodshed and carriage house, connecting with the barn beyond. The well, which is now some distance back from the house, was then under the kitchen, in which stood the pump, for drawing the water.

The cellar would seem to have been limited to the east end or was used in common by the occupants of the house. Its center was taken up by the huge stone foundation of the chimney. There is at hand an interesting record of the division of the estate of Abijah Gale in 1805. It is worth preserving for its uniqueness as well as for its specifications of the various parts of the house. "And having set off the East part of said dwelling house & cellar to said widow, we reserve for their heirs, the privilege to use the milk cellar and the East end of the house in common with said widow & the front chamber stairs to be improved in common with said wilow & said heirs & the fire place & ovens in kitchen to be used in common —also set to widow the privilege of passing . . . to the cellar, chamber, & garret stairs, also to the cheese room, dairy house & hot closet, also to pass to & from well at North part of house,—to lay her firewood in dooryard at South West part of house,—of passing by front of cyder house to & from her barn,—also to hogpen at North East side of cyder house."

Inside the house, the old corner posts and ceiling beams still show plainly. As a tavern it was the center of many interesting gatherings, as well as the stopping place of travelers

It is often referred to in Mr. Parkman's Diary. One noteworthy incident was that of Sept. 2, 1774. "This morning was ushered in with Alarms from every Quarter, to get ready & run down to Boston or Cambridge, the contents of the Magazine of Powder at Winter Hill had been carryd off. . . . 72 of our Neighbors marched from Gale's ('tis said) by break of day; and others are continually going. My young man goes in armed with them. . , . It is a day of peculiar anxiety & Distress! Such as we have not had."

Though this proved to be a false alarm, note that it occurred the fall before the battle at Lexington. The old tavern was on other occasions the rendezvous of the militia.

Mr. Parkman often called there. In April 1775, he "called at Mr. Gale's, partly to see old Mr. Gale and his wife, and to receive also a present of fine Carrotts."

References in the Diary show Mr. Gale was a leader in Church matters, and served on important committees. In Jan. 1789 he was appointed to assist in the ordination of Mr. Robinson as pastor—a notable occasion as there had been none such for 64 years.

The following from the "Gale Records," written by George Gale, L. L. D., of Galesville, Wisconsin, has been handed us by Mrs. Cyrus Gale of Northborough, and will be of interest in this connection:

"Abijah Gale of Westborough married June 23, 1748, Abigail Amsden of Westborough, to which town he immediately removed from Weston, and lived in what was afterward called "The Gale Tavern." Abijah entered the service of his "King" in June, 1756, in the "French and Indian war" and served through the most of that war and was in some of the hardest battles. In 1757 he was in that part of the company not surrendered to the French at Fort William Henry, and was marked as having, with 132 others in Col. Frye's regiment, deserted on the 12th of August, three days after the surrender of the fort. As they were never punished for the desertion, but Abijah re-entered the service the following spring, it was probably considered only as a "red tape" desertion, and really justifiable, under the circumstances.

The old iron soldier finally died June 18th, 1804, in peace, amidst his numerous family, so unostentatiously that the town records do not even mention the time of his death.

His first wife, Abigail, died Feb. 27, 1771, and he married Susannah Allen of

Weston, Nov. 14th of the same year, who died Jan. 14th, 1831, aged 91 years. She was a very smart woman, a tailoress, and went from house to house making clothes, and in her 90th year cut and made a suit of woolen clothes for one of her neighbors.

Mr Gale's will recites:

Abijah Gale of Westborough, Yeoman, being advanced in age, &c.

He dated his will April 16, 1804, and gave to his wife, Susanna, her dower of ⅓ of the estate, & one cow, $40 in money, one looking glass, one case of drawers and "40 dining chairs she brought with her," meaning, probably, at their marriage

2. Gives to his five sons, Nahum, Amsden, Lewis & Cyrus & David, all real & personal property except as follows:

To "Nahum, 1 Pew & horse stable at Meeting house" &c. ⅓ use of them to widow during her life.

To son, Elisha, $5, which, with what he had already given him, was his proportion.

To son, Isaac, $35 same as Elisha.

To daughter, Eunice, $100, half in furniture & balance in cash.

To daughter, Susannah, $100, same as Eunice.

To Abijah Nichols, deceased, heirs at law, $7.

To granddaughter Nancy, $50; probably daughter of Abijah Gale, Jr.

The will was proved and allowed Aug. 7, 1804, and Nahum appointed executor.

The inventory amounted to, real estate $6,166 and personal estate $933 19 being of the total sum of $7,000. This amount, with what he had already settled on his oldest children, indicates that he was one of the most wealthy men in town.

He was a hotel keeper, and kept a popular stopping place for judges and lawyers between Worcester and Boston; many anecdotes of which he used to tell in the latter part of his life. He was fond of jokes and tradition says that when his wife left one Sabbath for church, she instructed Abijah to "put the pot boiling for dinner," and sure enough he put the pot in a five pail kettle, filled the kettle with water and had the pot boiling in good earnest when the good wife returned.

Being a good business man, he was continually pressed with town offices, hence we find him constable in 1764; on the committee to hire a schoolmaster in 1768; surveyor of boards and shingles, and on a committee to put in four new pews in the church, in 1769; surveyor of highways in 1770; one of a committee of seven, in 1773, "to take into consideration ye rights as stated by the committee of Correspondence of ye town of Boston, & of ye infringements & violations of ye same." After naming the grievances of the Colonies, this committee say: "It appears that every member of this Committee, qualified to act in town affairs, should at all times have a proper sense of them, more especially as ye Future happiness of his Family, as well as himself, depends greatly on their being Removed. For no Dought ware tyranny is exercised, opposition becomes a Duty. As our fathers could, so can we plead our Loyalty, we have been and now are ready to spill our dearest blood in the defence of our King, Religion & Constitutional Laws. We cannot but look upon it as a hard trial, yea, greater than we can bear, if we cannot be said to give full proof of our Loyalty, otherwise than by sacrificing those Rights and Liberties, which we prize beyond life itself."

In the same year he was chairman of a committee to sell "Pue Spots" around the church In 1775, he was one of a committee of "Inspection & Observation" recommended by the Continental Congress. In 1777, he was chairman of a committee "to make a remonstrance to the General Court, concerning the state money being put on loan, &c." In 1778, he was chairman of a committee to consult together on the plan of Government sent out by Congress. He reported that: "We are of the opinion that the Protestant Religion is not duly guarded in said Constitution. Also, we think it might be well to acknowledge the Superintendence of Heaven in the Stile: by adding these words: (under God) after the words shall be, which remark we humbly submit to the town for acceptance."

The same year he was chairman of a committee "to give instruction to our Representative concerning ye Constitution;" and on another committee "to settle with those who had been in the military service of the United States;" and also moderator of the town meeting. In 1779, he was chairman of the selectmen, and the same the following year (an important office in those days.)

Seventeen children were born to him, six by his first wife, eleven by the second. Several of them lived to a ripe old age. Capt. Cyrus Gale of Northborough was 94 years, 11 months, when he died.

It is of interest to note this last named son, started forth from the old homestead in 1800, when but 15 years of age, with but $2 in pocket to seek his fortune, especially eager to earn money that he might contribute it toward the support of the family. He walked to Boston and applied at the old market for work. He went to live with one Isaac Davis at Roxbury and proved himself one of the most capable of lads.

After a few years he was able to carry on the business for himself.

"He was a provision dealer and wholesale and retail grocery merchant in Boston," writes one, "and during the war of 1812 captain of a company of militia in the city. In subsequent life Capt Gale has been postmaster, selectman and for 50 years justice of the peace. He has also been two terms a member of the Legislature and one term a member of the Governor's Council."

He was the father of the present Cyrus Gale, whose public spirited gifts of "The Gale Library," and of the Park and adjacent real estate on Mt. Assabet to his native town, have continued to honor the family name.

From the heirs of Abijah Gale the estate passed through various hands to Luther Chamberlain between 1829 and 1831. He sold, in June 13 of the latter year, the part on which stood the house to Pierpont Brigham

In 1836, the will of the latter, approved Nov. 7, gave to Widow Annah the income of the new farm of 75 acres and to the sons in law Charles Brigham, Jr., and Dexter Brigham, with their wives, "All money from the sales of the old farm"—which was on the east side of the highway—also to the Annah E. and Martha W., "the income of all property given my wife after she ceased to be my widow &c—their children to have the principle of said estate."

It was in 1862, that the barn was burned and the very next year, the barn and the ell and back part of the house were destroyed by fire. This necessitated the rebuilding of the roof and other parts, and in the process, the old garret and the back rooms in the second story were omitted.

In Feb. and Mar. 1863, the title of the estate including the so called "Gale

Place" passed to Dexter Brigham 2nd, from the various parties interested.

Later the same year the last named as guardian of Dexter P., Albert B. and Ella C Brigham, then minors, sold it to Charles M. Buck, who in 1864 sold the 'Gale Place" to Dennis Fitzpatrick The latter held it for over 20 years, and in 1895 sold it to J. J. Ryan, who conveyed it in 1903 to Jennie W. Nichols, the present owner, now Mrs. Otis A. Freeman.

S. INGERSOLL BRIANT.
November 1906.

The Thomas Whitney House.

On a little knoll in the southwesterly section of Westborough, on the North Grafton road and near the Grafton boundary, stands an old, weatherbeaten structure, grim, silent and alone. A narrow lane partially lined with lilacs leads from the highway to it. That the best of material and workmanship entered into its construction, that the hand of time has passed very gently over it. and that the elements have been especially kind, are evidenced by its state of preservation today, where the vandal's hand has not mutilated it. It is a monument to departed days and stands out upon the landscape as a historic picture of alternating lights and shades framed in the faraway past; the ell and shed antedating the revolution by considerably more than a quarter of a century. Guarded by majestic trees of ash, it seems a garrison from which the troops have been transferred, while the sentries still pace their beat. All over it, is written in legible characters, "Passing away," and over its front entrance we read in illuminated colors, the word "Veneration," for we venerate the old house for sake of him who placed it there, for them that have gone in and out of its portals, leaving the impress of their hurrying feet upon its thresholds and for the days of dear delight we have passed within its walls. Who erected the deserted house, in what year it was built, and what of them that have owned and occupied it are pertinent questionings and the best answer we are able to give we now offer.

We open the book of Time at page 1735 A. D., and among the records entered thereon find this:—"To all people to whom these presents shall come, greeting; know that I, Joseph Grout of the town of Westboro, county of Worcester in his majesty's province of Massachusetts Bay in New England, husbandman, for and in consideration of the sum of two hundred and fifty pounds in good current and lawful money of this province, to me in hand, well and truly, paid before the ensealing hereof by Thomas Whitney of ye town of Watertown in ye county of Middlesex in ye province of Massachusetts bay in New England before mentioned, husbandman, the receipt thereof I do hereby acknowledge and myself to be fully satisfied herewith as paid and contented, for every part and parcel thereof and do hereby exonerate, acquit and discharge him the said Thomas Whitney, his heirs, executors, administrators, and assigns forever by these presents have given, granted, bargained, sold, aliened conveyed and conformed, and by these presents do fully, freely and clearly and absolutely give, grant, bargain, sell, aliene, convey and confirm unto him the said Thomas Whitney, his heirs, executors, etc., a certain tract of land, containing seventy acres, be ye same more or less, with a dwelling house thereon.

The said land is situated, lying and being in the southeasterly part of ye town of Shrewsbury, county of Worcester, province of Mass. bay in New England and is bounded as follows: Beginning at the southeast corner with a crooked black oak tree marked, from thence running westerly partly by the land belonging to ye heirs of John Fay, Jr., late of Westboro, deceased, and partly by land formerly of Capt. Nathan Brigham of Marlboro' by marked trees till it comes to a red oak tree marked, at ye southwest corner, then turning northerly and running by ye land of Ebenezer Nurse to a pine tree marked, thence running to a stake and heap of stones at the northwest corner, then turning easterly by ye said Nurse his land, to a maple tree marked, thence turning to a stake and heap of stones, thence running to a great white oak tree marked, thence running to stake and heap of stones at the northeast corner, then turning southerly and running by ye land of Eleazer Pratt and from thence running to a chestnut tree staked and from thence running to the black oak tree first mentioned. To have and to hold the same premises with the dwelling house thereon and all that is whatsoever now standing, lying or growing therein and thereon Whereunto I, Joseph Grout and Mary Grout, wife of said Joseph, by her mark, have set our hands and seals this ninth day of April in ye year one thousand seven hundred and thirty five, in ye eight year of ye reign of our Sovereign Lord, George second, of Great Brittain, France and Ireland—King. Defender of faith, etc. Signed, sealed and delivered in presence of Isaiah Goodnow, Ebenezer Parkman, Francis Harrington, Nahum Ward. The tract of this conveyance, was in the "Shrewsbury Shoe," so called, and the house was a small, one story frame dwelling 26 ft. by 28 ft., facing the south, with a shed 13 ft. by 31 ft., attached, in which a small room was finished. In this room were two windows and a door. On the south side of the house were two rooms, kitchen and bedroom. Back of these or facing the highway, were the "best" room, pantry and "set kettle" room, which was later divided into two small rooms. From the kitchen, stairways led to the open chamber, through which one passed to the tiny furnished chamber over the set kettle room and to the cellar. The kitchen and "best" room were equipped with fireplaces, and the huge chimney of that day, occupied quite a part of the floor space.

There are good reasons for belief that the erection of the house was about 1730. Mr. Thomas Whitney, the purchaser, was the third generation from John Whitney born in England, 1589, who settled in Watertown, 1635, and died there June 1, 1673. Mr. Thomas Whitney was born 1695 in Watertown and baptized in the Second church of that place Jan. 28, 1699, by Rev. Mr. Angier. He was a farmer and had learned the wheelwright business from his father, Mr. Eleazer Whitney. At the acquisition of his new property he was the father of six children, four boys and two girls; the eldest, Eleazer, born Nov. 30, 1720, the youngest, Susannah, born May 17, 1729.

Of this Mr. Thomas Whitney, our great, great grandsire, our knowledge is very limited. That he was an energetic, ambitious man, jovial and blunt, we have been assured. That he delved out a living among the rocks of his mowings and fields is certain. That he was a strict disciplinarian has come down through the generations. He died May 8, 1748, aged 53 years.

Of his estate we find the following division, May 27, 1748, approved by court Aug. 10, 1748: "Twenty acres in Shrewsbury, * * * * has a small dwelling house thereon and some orchard thereon which said land with the house and improvements thereon we have allowed and appraised at one hundred pounds. We have set out to Hannah, the widdow, 4 acres with the dwelling house and some orchard. The said 4 acres are in the East side of the aforesaid 20 acres. appraised at £33,6s,4d.

The remaining 16 acres valued at £66, 13s, 4d, (not being capable of deviding too & amongst the heirs without spiling the same) we have set it off to Thomas, the second son, (the eldest son having refused to have it set off to him) and have ordered the said Thomas to pay out of the said estate the following: To his brother Eleazer, the oldest son, £22, 4s, 5d; to Nathan, the youngest, £11, 2s, 2d, 2f; to sister Hannah, married to Ebenezer Sanders, £11, 2s, 2d, 2f, and to his youngest sister, Susannah, £11, 2s, 3d, 2f."

Fifteen acres of the purchase Mr. Thomas Whitney, senior, had conveyed by deed to his son Thomas, July 9, 1747, and thirty acres to Mr. Benjamin Fay Nov. 3, 1747,

Of Mrs. Hannah Smith Whitney, whom he married July 1, 1720, we know she was one of New England's colonial dames, who were proverbial for immaculateness, proficiency in the culinary art and devotion to their families and home interests. She was not a club woman, The time of her death is unknown, as is the resting place of both herself and her husband, but as some of their descendants sleep in the old cemetery at South Shrewsbury it is probable that among the graves whose headstones have fallen and become indecipherable, are theirs.

Of the children, Eleazer, the eldest, died at 18. Hannah married Ebenezer Sanders. Thomas, our great grandsire, born Sept. 3 1722, married Anna Gould Feb. 24, 1753, and took her to the old house as a bride He was a frugal temperate man, banishing from his board, save on extra occasions, all forms of intoxicants. Tobacco was his abhorrence and he refused to sit by the side of a user of it at any time or place. Like his father, he was a good farmer and being of an inquiring turn of mind, his time and attention were somewhat divided between the improvement of his acres and bee culture, his one hive giving ample opportunity for study of the habits and haunts of the bee, while rearing the cellular house and storing therein the winter's food. At swarming, however, the bees decided to make their new home in the spacious chimney and to call them from their retreat, as a last resort, a bundle of straw was lighted on the hearth. This unlooked for result of his labors robbed Mr. Whitney of all desire for further experience with bees.

When the news of Paul Revere's midnight ride and the message he bore, reached his ears, his patriotism was aroused and at a date unknown he was enrolled as a private in Capt. John Maynard's company of staunch Shrewsburians, under Col. Job Cushing, son of the pastor of the Congregational church of that town from 1723 to 1760. Of his service we find this entry: "The company marched to Hadley by order of Col. Denny on an alarm at Bennington. They marched 60 miles in three days." He was honorably discharged Aug. 23, 1777.

That he had a tenacious love for old friends and places is evidenced in his declination to be annexed to Westborough, although the annexation of 1762 left him and his little 40 acres as an island, completely surrounded by Westborough. His desire was to die as he had lived,—a citizen of Shrewsbury. He united with the Congregational church of that town in 1784 That our great grandmother also united with that church is a matter of fact. May 11, 1807, she united by letter with the church in Westborough.

Like her immaculate mother-in-law she was a wondrous housekeeper. Two nights a week, when the moon was at its full, both she and our great grandsire sat up all night, she spinning and weaving, he shelling corn on a shovel and such other work as the season might invite. Fortunately they were not in an apartment house. Truly, they were an industrious, thrifty, hardy race.

Mr. Whitney died April 25, 1806, aged 84 years. His wife died August 10, 1812, and both are presumably buried in the old cemetery at South Shrewsbury.

Of their six children, Timothy, born Nov 29, 1753, was, like his father, patriotic and enlisted in Capt. Joseph Warren's company, leaving wife and three months old son, in Sept , 1777, one month after his father's discharge, and was commissioned lieutenant. His name stands on the honor roll hung on the wall of the Shrewsbury public library. He married Miss Phebe Reed and there we lose trace of him.

Sarah, born Nov. 21, 1756, married Jonas Hemenway of Shrewsbury Feb. 28, 1790, and died Sept. 8, 1827, aged 71.

Anna, born May 24, 1764, married Silas Wheelock, also of Shrewsbury, on her 19th birthday, and died Feb. 23, 1842, aged 78.

John Smith Whitney, born Dec. 4, 1768, married Susanna Knowlton, sister of Judge Knowlton, one of Massachusetts' earliest leaders of the bar, Feb. 24, 1794, and died in the west. He was the father of Joseph Hastings Whitney, late resident of this town.

Jonah, youngest of the family, born Aug. 25, 1771, died Oct. 3, 1810, aged 39, being killed while moving a building.

Elijah, our grandsire, born April 21, 1761, married Miss Mindwell Hardy, a cousin of the father of Mr. William F. and the late Susan M. Hardy, May 29, 1785. We quote from the Whitney genealogy: "Elijah Whitney was a handsome man and an excellent farmer and his father, Thomas, seems to have relied mainly upon him in business matters. When 'the Shoe,' in 1762, was annexed to Westboro Thomas, the father, desired to remain a citizen of Shrewsbury, and his request was granted; he, however, yielded to Elijah's request March 12, 1793, and the farm, which had become Elijah's property, was annexed to Westboro." In reality, Elijah rebelled against longer travelling on rackets unnecessary miles over impassable roads to attend religious services or municipal gatherings. That he was a church-going man is inferential by his purchase, April 8, 1799, from Mr. Eli Whitney of "A certain Pew in the publick Meeting House in Said Westborough, and is Situate, Standing and being between Joseph Harrington's pew & Simeon Bellow's Pew, and is on the South side, or front of said Meeting house and is a wall Pew so called Under the Galleries." This deed was acknowledged before Elijah Brigham, Jus. Pacis, and witnessed by Moses Wheelock and Nathaniel Andrews. "He was kind to his children and allowed his son, Elijah, to leave his trade and pursue a course at college and graduate as a learned man. His comparatively early death was a sad blow to his sons who were just passing into manhood. He was frugal and careful in his life and left a fair amount of real estate to be divided between his children."

To the genealogical record we add the testimony of one of his contemporaries, Mr. Moses Grout: "He possessed great executive ability and was persistently sought for town offices, all of which he declined, giving his time and undivided attention to the rearing of his large family and farm work. His fields of corn were his pride and many of his townsmen depended upon him for their spring planting."

Of him, also, we are told that the hours of two nights a week, at the full moon, were utilized in the advancement of such interests as seemed to demand immediate attention, and his wife with her busy fingers kept him company, which disposes of any question that might arise concerning his membership in any "union," save the felicitous domestic one, and proves her a scion of a "Hardy" race at least. Fortunately that over-plus of energy was not bequeathed to later generations. Her bridal outfit, apparel, table and bed linen were the work of her own hands. Her feather bed, pillows and bolster were her own handiwork, from the plucking of the geese to the last stitch therein; (the furnishings, not the geese.)

Specimens of her spinning, weaving and emboidery are still in existence.

One brave feat of hers has come to us. Soon after her widowhood two cows became quarrelsome and in their combat fell with horns interlocked. In the struggle for separation one was thrown on her back with the long slender horns deep set in the sward. Realizing her peril, the brave woman of petite figure, seized the head and released the frantic animal.

The executive ability of this Daughter of the Revolution and French and Indian war as well, was marvelous and shown in the rearing of her 11 children, especially after her widowhood, at which time the youngest was but seven years old I quote the late Mrs Theodore F. Brigham: "Her cooking was par excellence and none could rival her in the housewifely art. It was a genuine delight to visit there, as none need fear to wear their best."

The trees which stand as sentries, guarding the old house of so many cherished memories, were planted by her hands, while still a bride, and have withstood the shocks and storms of 120 years. She was received into the Congregational church May 24, 1818.

The exact date of the erection of the main part of the homestead we regret our inability to determine. There is a difference of opinion concerning it, its erection being accredited to both Mr. Thomas Whitney and Mr. Elijah Whitney. We give all that has come to us. In a letter from the late Susan M. Hardy we find "that Mr. Thomas Whitney's children and Mr. Elijah Whitney's children, born previous to 1793, were born in Shrewsbury, while those born after that date were born in Westborough, and yet they were all born in the same house." From another distant relative we have the corroboration of this affirmation, and knowing Miss Hardy's punctilliousness in all matters, we had assumed "the same house" referred to the structure of today, no discrimination being made. From our father and his youngest sister we learned of the housewarming, with the name of one person of lisping tongue and eccentricity of speech, who was present. Reference to the church manual reveals the fact that a person of that name was received into membership in 1749. A relative, our senior, has given the opinion that it was built by Mr. Elijah Whitney.

During the past summer the house has been twice inspected by masterbuilders, the specialty of one being the taking down and repairing of old buildings. His judgment was that it was built not later than 1765. The other gave us his opinion that about 50 years elapsed between the building of the two structures, which, granting the old dwelling to have been erected in 1730, would give a date of 1780 for the addition, at which time Mr. Elijah Whitney was but nineteen years of age. If Mr. Thomas Whitney was the builder, it was in the later years of his ownership, and if Mr. Elijah Whitney, in the early days of his possession. We accordingly give the date as between 1765 and 1785, the advantage of building permits being clearly demonstrated.

From our father we learn that it was built by one Asa Munroe,

> But whence he came to earn his fame
> We're sure we cannot tell.
> This we do know, that time doth show
> He did his work right well.

At the "raising", Mr. Whitney's neighbors and friends were present, to assist in placing the massive frame in position, and when it was upright, bread and butter, cheese and flip were served. The "minister" also was present and invoked a divine blessing on the inmates of the old house, those who should come after them, the laborers and the permanency of the new structure. That the long prayer has been answered in one particular the deserted house bears daily evidence.

Its exterior is after the manner of construction of that day, its hand-made window frames being a solid piece of timber. It is a two story structure, with one room on each side of the front door, which opens to a small entry. The "southroom" has three windows, two on the west or front, one facing south, and two doors, one opening on the yard, the other to a narrow hall leading to the kitchen. The walls are wainscotted. In one corner is the brick oven, evidencing it was designed for the living room. The "north room" has five windows, two west, two north and one east. The dentilated frieze bespeaks the 'best room." Over these rooms are the chambers, the north chamber being divided into halves making two rooms over the one below. Four of these rooms have fireplaces; closets and cupboards of various sizes are in all the rooms. In the center stands the chimney of that day. After the addition was built, the "best room" of the dwelling, became the "middle room," with its highboy, and in winter the high posted mahogany bedstead, and the bedroom was divided into two pantries. It is a solid structure, severe in outline, and designed to weather the storms of centuries And that it will fulfil the intent of its builder seems a foregone conclusion. And as we wander through the deserted rooms, comes the thought, what of them who have called the house home?

Mr. Elijah Whitney died there Aug. 24, 1817, aged 56 years. By his will dated Sept. 28, 1812, he left the home farm to his wife while she remained his widow. Mrs. Whitney died April 28. 1853, aged 89¼ years. Both sleep in Midland cemetery.

Of the eleven children; Azubah, born Oct. 13, 1785, married Joel Adams of Northbridge and was buried there. She died June 29, 1835, aged 49 years, Nahum born Jan. 7, 1788, married Susanna, sister of Joel Adams, and died Dec. 22. 1843, aged 55, and was laid in Midland. Asenath, born March 12, 1790, married Noyes Bryant, father of the late Alfred Bryant and sleeps in Midland. Joel, born May 12, 1792, married Ebial Nason, and his resting place is unknown. David, the father of Mrs. Jasper Fay, born June 9, 1795, was the eldest one within our memory. He was a whole-souled, genial gentleman, a farmer, and his fields and meadows attested his ability, industry and thrift. He married Miss Samaria Wheeler, and with her spent his later years in Grafton where he died Dec. 12, 1861, aged 66¼ years. Mrs. Whitney died May 19, 1892 aged 90¼ years. Both lie in Midland. Levi saw scarcely two months of life and was laid in the family lot.

Elijah, the central star of the human constellation and the only one who rose to prominence, was born Nov. 26, 1798. He was of fine physique, standing six feet three and well proportioned. Being of a studious nature he took a course in Brown University, then at Yale and later at Union college, graduating in 1852 Immediately he opened an academy at Stockbridge, Mass., from which he graduated Cyrus W. Field. Later he studied and taught in Lane Seminary, Cincinnati, with Dr. Lyman Beecher and was ordained to the gospel ministry at Chenango, N Y., in 1837. For seventeen years he was engaged in pastoral work, when losing his voice, he studied medicine at Syracuse medical college and in 1852 removed to New York city, which he made his permanent home and became a regular practitioner, continuing in active practice till his ninetieth year. He was twice married, to Miss Cornelia L. Pratt and later to Wealthy Bryant. Among his closer friends he numbered Webster, Clay, Calhoun, Henry Ward Beecher and many others of note. Among his literary productions was a treatise on yellow fever, and a book on Asiatic cholera. He was a wide lecturer on temperance and moral reform, and delivered a lecture in Grand Union hall in his eighty-fifth year, and again manifested his vigor, both mental and physical, by an address in the Academy of Anthropology on his ninetieth anniversary. During the civil war he was a surgeon under Col. Hunter. One incident of his boyhood we give in his own language: "From the crane in the old fireplace, was suspended a huge iron pot and I was curious to know more concerning its contents. My curiosity led me to lean over the pot for a deep inhalation of the strong odor, and leaning too far, the pot tipped toward me, and the soup apparently went through me, as the smarting was about equal on both sides. The trapdoor of my clothing had suddenly swung on its hinges and there appeared to be a plentitude of shingles flying in mid-air." He was a member of Madison Square Presbytarian church, and died Apr. 7, 1892, aged 93¼ years. He was buried from Union Tabernacle and sleeps in Woodlawn.

Mindwell Clarinda, eighth child, married James Searl, uncle of Mr. Uriah Searles,and took him to the old house as a bridegroom. Under her superintendence the former standard of excellence in all departments was maintained.

Our memories of the house are with her as its mistress. She was admitted to the church Dec. 8, 1822, and died in North Grafton, Nov. 26, 1877, aged 76½ years. Both she and her husband sleep in Midland.

Orestes died at the age of 23 and lies in the family lot.

Dexter Osborne, youngest of the family, born Sept. 17, 1809, was the wit of the family, seeing all things in their most ludicrous light and taking a more philosophical view of adversity and perversity than was usual with the Whitneys. He was by occupation a mechanic. He married Catherine Newton and later Mrs. Lavinia Kanuse. He died Nov. 8, 1875, aged 66 years, in Webster, where he was buried.

Mr. Daniel Whitney, tenth of the eleven children, was the one we knew best. For thirty-three years we called him father. Five feet eleven in height, straight as an arrow, honorable in the strictest sense of the term, temperate, genial, yet dignified in manner to a fault. He was a farmer and his hobby was fine stock, and finer animals than were stalled in his barn it would be difficult to find outside the thoroughbred. His barn was swept twice daily and no lantern was needed to locate any part of his farm paraphernalia. His judgment in the purchase and exchange of animals was widely sought and rarely proved erroneous. The stone walls that bounded his acres were his pride, laid by his own hands.

On Sept. 2, 1824, he saw Lafayette at Worcester, as he was on his way from Boston to New York.

At the age of twenty he was commissioned cornet in a Regiment of Cavalry, 2d Brigade, Sixth Division, Aug. 20, 1827. He was honorably discharged July 7, 1828. His inherent pride was evidenced, when in carrying the standard on the muster field, he desired the finest mount to be found and locating a handsome black stallion at Taunton, drove over in a chaise, paid five dollars per day for use of the animal and rode him home. He was the cynosure of all eyes in more ways than one. The horse was unaccustomed to martial music and, being a mettled steed, the rider circled the field at a pace and in a manner widely at variance with his usual dignity and not at all in accord with the requirements of the occasion. He, however, reached the head of the line in ample time to lead in the evolutions. It was his first and last horse race!

Among the friends he held in lifelong remembrance were Col. Josiah Brigham, Major Gleason, Harrison O. Fay. John A. Fayerweather, Dean Fisher, Joel Andrews and Jonas Longley, and we might add Miss Beulah Peters and Miss Salome White.

April 11, 1830, he united with the Congregational church, and in 1848 removed to Grafton, with the full intent of returning to his native place for his declining years In this he was disappointed and died in Grafton April 27, 1881, aged 74, and sleeps in Midland with his two wives, Miss Nancy B. Newton of Westboro and Miss Sarah S. Fisk of Shelburne, one of the pupils of Miss Lyon at Mt. Holyoke.

The last birth in this house was Adaline A. Whitney April 20, 1810, daughter of Nahum Whitney, and fourth generation from the first Mr. Thomas Whitney.

The last Whitney occupant was Mrs. Mindwell Searl, who transferred the property to Mr. John B. Adams, son of her elder sister, April 23, 1866, although she remained there till the following year. April 16, 1867, Mr. Adams deeded the farm to Mr. Jasper Fay, and July 23, 1879, Mr. Fay transferred it back to

Mr. Adams of Springfield, the last change the Registry of Deeds records.

During the years last mentioned, the original windows, with their 7x9 panes were replaced by more modern four-lighted ones, giving it somewhat the appearance of a colonial dame who has outlived her time and being more ambitious than discreet, has aped the attire of a later generation in the adoption of rimless eye glasses. And with fragrant memories of the past, we quietly close the door of the deserted house and leave it to the leveling hand of Time.

And for those guardians of our Past,
Waifs on time's human ocean cast,
Descendants of an alien soil,
Inured to hardship and to toil,
We claim but this: They came and went,
Each on one common purpose bent,
To do the very best they knew,
To every trust to prove them true,
The sacrificial flame to feed,
To help a brother if he need,
The Lord to honor, love, revere,
And trace a record bright and clear.
And if they missed the mark in aught,
Who of himself, can say it not?
And thus they wrought beyond their ken,
In life and death, God's noblemen.

ESTHER M. HOWELL.

Worcester, Dec. 12, 1906.

INDEX

Adams, Joel, 64.
    John B., 66.
    Susanna, 64.
Allen, Susanna, 56.
Ames, Levi, 25.
Amsden, Abigail, 54, 55.
    Isaac, 54.
    Jacob, 54.
    Lydia, 54.
Andrews, Joel, 65.
    Nathaniel, 62.
    Rhoda, 17.
    Thomas, 45.
    Thos. Elliot, 45.
Arnold, Capt. Benedict, 37.
Bailey, Mrs, Elizabeth S., 45.
    Samuel K., 45.
    Mrs. Samuel R , 45.
Baker, Edward, 25, 26, 33-35.
    Joseph, 11.
Baldwin, C. C., 41.
    Mrs., 25.
Bannister, G. L., 30.
Baptists, 45, 51, 52.
Bass, Gillam, 25.
Batherick, Jonathan, 28.
    Solomon, 17.
Baverick, David, 33.
Bayley, Mrs., 13.
Beaman, Dea., 51.
    Eleazar, 54.
Beaton, John, 25, 50.
Beers, Richard, 12.
Bellows, Hannah, 44.
    Simeon, 62.

Bigelow, Timothy, 10.
Billings, Mrs., 42.
Bishop, R. F., 18.
Bixby, Lovett, 18.
Blake, M. Horatio, 13.
Bond, Joseph, 25, 35.
Boynton, Mrs. Reuben, 52.
Breck, Hannah, 41.
Brigham, Albert B., 58.
    Anna, 7, 9, 46.
    Mrs. Anna, 5, 57.
    Annah E , 57.
    Charles, 57.
    Dexter, 57.
    Dexter, 2nd., 58.
    Dexter, P., 58.
    Edmund, 36.
    Elijah. 28, 29, 62.
    Ella C , 58.
    Ephraim, 34.
    Gershom, Family, 48-50.
    John, 5, 39.
    Martha W., 57.
    Moses, 40.
    Nathan, 21, 25, 39, 40, 48, 59.
    Phinehas, 35.
    Pierpont, 57.
    Samuel, 3, 6, 54.
    Sarah, 40.
    Susannah, 25-28.
    Theodore F., 62.
    Thomas, 39, 48, 49.
Brittan, Mrs. Lydia M., 45, 53.
Broaders, Hiram, 9, 47.
    Hiram L., 47.

Broaders, Jacob, 46, 47.
Brown, N. Porter, 18.
Bryant, Alfred, 64.
    Noyes, 64.
    Wealthy, 64.
Buck, Charles M., 58.
Bullard, Martin, 18.
Bumpso, Sam, 33.
Burnap, A J., 30.
Burnham, G H., 12.
    Susanna, 51.
Carter, Nehemiah, 45.
Cary, Arthur, 34.
Chamberlain, John, 46.
    Joshua, 25.
    Luther, 57.
    Nathaniel, 35.
Champney, Hannah, 20.
    Major, 28.
    Mary, 20, 24, 42.
    Samuel, 20.
Child, Mrs Emily A., 53.
Clark, Ben, 25.
    Mrs., 52.
Cobb, John, 47.
Coburn, W. A., 12.
Cook, Cornelius, 44, 45.
Costello, J T., 12.
Crcnican, Mrs. B. T., 30.
    Patrick, 30.
Cullock, Joseph, 26.
Curtis, Dr. William, 21, 23.
Cushing, Rev. Job, 31.
    Capt. Job, 61.
Davenport, A., 30.
Davis, Mrs. G. C., 42.
    Isaac, Family, 6, 8, 9, 46-48, 57.
Death, Patty, 5.
Denny, Augusta M., 24, 27.
    George, 27.
    Col., 61.
    Robert B., 27.
Dickinson, William, 23.
Dudley, Mrs. Annette B., 30.
Eaton, Gov. Theophilus, 39.
Edwards, Daniel, 32.
    Rev. Jonathan, 32, 51.

Elmer, Rev. Daniel, 16.
Fay, Benjamin, 34, 60.
    Cyrus, 12.
    Jasper, 64, 65.
    Jeduthan, 29.
    John, 26, 34, 35, 39, 59.
    Samuel, 17, 26, 39.
    Solomon T., 45.
    Stephen, 38.
Ferguson, G. A., 41.
Field, Cyrus W., 64.
Fields, Mrs. Grace M., 51.
Fisher, Dean, 65.
    Rev. H. P., 18.
    Mr., 25, 26.
    Nathan, 36.
Fisk, Sarah S., 65.
Fitzpatrick, Dennis, 58.
Flagg, Hannah, 15.
Forbes, Daniel, 13, 15.
    Elisha, 12, 15.
    Jonathan, Family, 15, 16, 37-43.
Forbush, Daniel, 16, 17, 43.
    Samuel, Family, 15-19, 42, 44.
    Thomas, Family, 16, 17, 43-45.
Freeman, Mrs. Otis A., 58.
Gage, Gov., 35.
Gale, Abijah, Family, 34, 51, 53-58.
Gibbs, Jacob, 34.
Gleason, Mr., 49.
Goddard, L. M., 39.
Goodnow, Isaiah, 59.
Gould, Anna, 60.
    Mrs. Sarah F., 43.
Grout, Eliza, 51.
    Jonathan, 34.
    Joseph, 40, 58, 59.
    Mary, 59.
    Mehetabel, 40.
    Moses, 62.
    Seth, 51.
    Susan, 51.
Haley, Patrick, 45.
Hancock, Mr., 25.
Hardy, Constantine, 4.
    Hannah, 49.
    Lucy, 49.

Hardy, Mindwell, 61.
    Susan M , 61-63.
    William F., 61.
Harrington, Edmund, 18.
    Francis, 59.
    Joseph, 33, 62.
    Rebecca, 13.
    Mrs. Sally, 18.
    Samuel, 33.
Harris, Rufus, 30.
Haskell, Family, 50-53.
Hawes, James, 35, 36, 45, 52, 53.
    Mary L., 53.
Hemenway, Jonas, 61.
Hills, David, 25.
Holbrook, Daniel, 51, 52.
    Levi, 51.
Holmes, R. G., 23.
Holyoke, President, 31, 32.
How, Samuel, 12.
Howe, A. M., 30.
    Luke, 18.
    Silas, 18.
Hunter, Col., 64.
Hutchinson, Gov., 35.
Jack Straw Hill, 12, 13.
Johnson, G. H., 47.
    Nathan, 10,
Judson, Rev. Adoniram, 23.
Kanuse, Lavinia, 65.
Keene, Joseph, 34, 35.
Kelly, Mrs., 25.
Kittredge, Rev. C. B., 39, 40.
    C. Brigham, 40, 41.
Knowlton, Judge, 61.
    N. M., 38.
    Susanna, 61.
Lamson, Mr., 28.
Lane, Michael, 21.
Leach, Mrs. Maria D. P., 30.
Leland, Orlando, 23.
Library, started, 25.
Lloyd, Dr. James, 11.
Longfellow, Messrs., 51.
Lock, President, 34.
Loring, Joshua, 7.
Lovell, Edwin H., 23.

Lyman School, 3, 6, 18, 47.
McCorry, C. E. S., 12.
McTaggert Farm, 40.
Maynard, Amasa, 47.
    Antipas, 4, 9, 46.
    Betty, 47.
    Dorothy, 46, 47.
    John, 3, 4, 7-9, 20, 21, 61.
    Phinehas, 46, 47.
    Stephen, Family, 3-12, 33, 35,
        42, 43, 46.
Mellen, Mr., 34.
Memorial Cemetery, 7, 21, 23, 40, 42, 50-52.
Midland Cemetery, 64, 65.
Miller, Barnabas, 13.
    James, 13.
Mills, Rev. Edward, 23.
Morse, Mr., 26.
    Seth, 33, 36.
Munroe, Asa, 63.
Nason, Ebial, 64.
    G. W., 12.
Nestor, John and Anne, 12.
Newton, Barnabas, 34, 35.
    Catherine, 65.
    Josiah, 4.
    Moses, 15.
    Nancy B., 65.
Nichols, Fortunatus, 11, 47.
    Joseph, 11.
    Walter F., 49.
Nurse, Ebenezer, 59.
    Moses, 28, 34.
Oak, Nathaniel, 16.
Parker, Tim., 34.
Parkman, Breck, Family, 13, 24-30, 35-37, 41.
    Charles B., 41.
    Diary, 4-7, 14, 15, 17, 20-22, 24-29, 31-37, 41-44, 46, 47, 49, 55.
    Rev. Ebenezer, Family, 3, 16, 17, 19-29, 35, 40, 41, 43, 49, 50.
    Rev. Francis, 41, 42.
    Mrs. Hannah, 11, 14, 24, 31, 41, 46.

Parkman, Mrs. Mary, 20, 24.
Pennell, Mr., 33.
Percy, Earl, 36.
Perriman, Rebecca, 44.
Peters, Beulah, 65.
    Lovett, 18.
    Onslow, 45.
Philip, King, 16.
Pierce, Mrs. E. T., 23.
Pierpont, Rev. James, 32, 41.
Pitkin, Col. George, 37.
Pluff, Louis, 12.
Pratt, Cornelia L., 64.
    Eleazar, 59.
Prescott, J. F., 12.
Reed, Phebe, 61.
Restorationists, 18.
Revolution, 8, 9, 10, 17.
Rice, Abigail, 16.
    Calvin, 47.
    Dinah, 40.
    Dorcas, 44.
    Dorothy, 46.
    Hannah, 15.
    Jonas & Lewis, 28.
    Mary, 49.
    Perez, 12.
    Seth, 46.
    Silas, 40.
    Thomas, 12.
    Timothy, 40.
Robinson, Rev. John, 28, 55.
Rockwood, Rev. E., 22, 28.
Ryan, J. J., 58.
Salsbury, Stephen, 34.
Sanders, Ebenezer, 60.
Searl, James, 65.
    Mrs. Mindwell, 65, 66.
Sever, Moses, 26,
Shattuck, Isaac, 13, 19.
Smith, Dr., 43.
    Joseph, 23.
Snow, Mrs. Elizabeth W., 40,
    Jacob, 25.
Spring, Mr., 25, 26.
Stearns, Elam, 18.
Stevens, W. R., 45.
Steward, Daniel, 47.

Stone, Bela J., 7.
Stowe, David, 28.
Taft, Cora, 23.
Tainter, Simon, Family, 12—15, 21, 31, 40.
Taynter, Joseph, 13.
Temple, Richard, 34.
Tenny, Abel, 34.
Thomas, Rowland, 32.
Tomblin, Dea., 6, 46.
Townshend, Nathan, 34.
Tuckerman, Mrs. Edward, 43.
Turnpike, Bos. & Worc., 17.
Tyler, Dr. John E., 24, 27, 28.
Wadsworth, Cyrus, 12,
    John, 12, 15,
    Mrs. Persis, 12, 13.
    Mrs. S. Maria, 13.
Waldo, Daniel, 45.
Ward, Gen. Artemas, 21, 23.
    Nahum, 59.
Ware, Asa, 26.
    Beriah, 47.
Warren, Abner, 53.
    Achsah, 53.
    Joseph, 61.
    Mrs, 14.
    John, 18.
Warrin, Aaron, 27.
    Timothy, 50.
Wesson, Silas, 18.
Wheeler, Samaria, 64.
Wheelock, Lydia, 52.
    Moses, 52, 53, 62.
    Silas, 61.
White, Abbie, 26.
Whitney, Thomas, Family, 58—66.
    Eli, 13, 62.
    Rev. Peter, 27, 46.
    Thomas, 36.
Willard, Benjamin, 26.
Winchester, Cousin, 31.
Wood, Hannah, 15.
Woods, Abigail, 26.
    Dea. Benjamin, 25—27, 34, 37, 49.
York, Alva W., 12.

www.ingramcontent.com/pod-product-compliance
Lightning Source LLC
LaVergne TN
LVHW051158080426
835508LV00021B/2698